THE HERBAL BED

THE HERBAL BED

by Peter Whelan

WARNER/CHAPPELL PLAYS

LONDON

A Warner Music Group Company

THE HERBAL BED
First published in 1996
by Warner/Chappell Plays Ltd
129 Park Street, London W1Y 3FA

Copyright © 1996 by Peter Whelan
Reprinted 1997 (twice)

The author asserts his moral right to be identified as the author of the work.

ISBN 0 85676 223 7

This play is protected by Copyright. According to Copyright Law, no public
performance or reading of a protected play or part of that play may be given without
prior authorization from Warner/Chappell Plays Ltd., as agent for the Copyright
Owners.

From time to time it is necessary to restrict or even withdraw the rights of certain plays.
**It is therefore essential to check with us before making a commitment to produce a
play.**

NO PERFORMANCE MAY BE GIVEN WITHOUT A LICENCE

AMATEUR PRODUCTIONS
Royalties are due at least fourteen days prior to the first performance. A royalty
quotation will be issued upon receipt of the following details:

Name of Licensee
Play Title
Place of Performance
Dates and Number of Performances
Audience Capacity
Ticket Prices

PROFESSIONAL PRODUCTIONS
All enquiries regarding professional rights should be addressed to The Agency
(London) Ltd, 24 Pottery Lane, Holland Park, London W11 4LZ.

OVERSEAS PRODUCTIONS
Applications for productions overseas should be addressed to our local authorized
agents. Further details are listed in our catalogue of plays, published every two years,
or available from Warner/Chappell Plays at the address above.

CONDITIONS OF SALE
This book is sold subject to the condition that it shall not by way of trade or otherwise
be re-sold, hired out, circulated or distributed without prior consent of the Publisher.
**Reproduction of the text either in whole or part and by any means is strictly
forbidden.**

Printed by Commercial Colour Press Plc, London E7

THE HERBAL BED was first performed by the Royal Shakespeare Company at The Other Place, Stratford Upon Avon, on 8th May, 1996 with the following cast:

JOHN HALL	Liam Cunningham
SUSANNA HALL	Teresa Banham
ELIZABETH HALL	Charlotte Jones/Olivia Jacob
HESTER FLETCHER	Jay McInnes
RAFE SMITH	Joseph Fiennes
JACK LANE	David Tennant
BISHOP PARRY	Raymond Bowers
BARNABUS GOCHE	Stephen Boxer

Directed by Michael Attenborough
Designed by Robert Jones
Lighting designed by Alan Burrett
Music by Adrian Johnston
Fight by Terry King
Music Director Michael Tubbs
Sound by Tim Oliver
Dialect Coach Charmian Hoare
Company voice work Barbara Houseman and Andrew Wade

Stage Manager Jon Ormrod
Deputy Stage Manager Suzi Blakey
Assistant Stage Manager Thea Jones

This production was financially supported by

CAST OF CHARACTERS

Rafe Smith, a haberdasher

Hester Fletcher, a servant

Jack Lane, a young gentleman

Bishop Parry of Worcester

John Hall, physician of Stratford-upon-Avon

Susanna, his wife

Barnabus Goche, Vicar-General

Elizabeth Hall, the Hall's daughter

The action takes place in the garden of John Hall's house in Stratford-upon-Avon, and in Worcester Cathedral during the summer of 1613.

ACT ONE

The garden of DOCTOR HALL'S *house (Hall's Croft, as it stands today), a substantial half-timbered two storey residence in Stratford-upon-Avon.*

The doctor's house contains its own dispensary where the mainly herbal prescriptions are prepared. The interior of the back room of the dispensary, opening into the garden is visible to us. Other parts of the house are glimpsed from the outside only. The garden is bordered by a high stone wall. There is a gate to one side.

Many of the herbs needed for the prescriptions are grown in abundance, with stone paths between the beds. They are grown in an orderly fashion, each species in its appropriate area. In the dispensary are the mortars and pestles for grinding the herbs and a small furnace for breaking down minerals.

It is June, 1613. A fine, pleasing day . . . high, racing clouds and blossom flying.

As the scene begins we discover RAFE SMITH *standing still among the herbs staring towards the house. From inside a faint murmur of voices as the* BISHOP *leads Dr Hall's household in prayer.* RAFE, *a haberdasher, soberly dressed, has brought a satchel of samples to show. It lies unopened on the garden bench.*

He has the manner of a man who does not belong. He wonders whether to go, but is inwardly compelled to stay. He calms himself by touching some stems of flowering herb with a gentle, loving motion, as though thinking of someone.

Suddenly HESTER *hurries out by the back door with a jug of beer and some food.*

HESTER   We couldn't come out sir! We knew you'd
                come but we couldn't stir!

RAFE   Who's talking in there?

HESTER	You don't know? Didn't you see his people in the street?
RAFE	I came in at the side . . .
HESTER	It's the Bishop of Worcester! He's blessing the doctor!
RAFE	What?
HESTER	It's surprised us all! He's passing through. And so many with him . . .
RAFE	I'll go . . . I've brought the doctor's hat. I'll leave it.
HESTER	She wants you to stay, sir . . .
RAFE	Tell her I'll come tomorrow . . .
HESTER	Oh sir . . . we haven't seen you in over a week! He'll be gone soon. Apparently he was setting off for Alcester and he said, "I won't go another yard till I've given Dr Hall a blessing." The doctor's treated him so often you see. No, no . . . stay! He'll have to be gone. He's said he'd be gone. Well don't be silly. Stay sir, please! She's going to give you an order, I know she is. Here's some beer and seed cakes and watercress. (*More personally.*) Don't go . . . will you?
RAFE	I don't want to meet a bishop.
HESTER	Now, now . . .
RAFE	I won't bow.
HESTER	Sssh!
RAFE	I won't bow to him. I won't bow and scrape to these people!

(*Enter* JACK LANE, *sweaty from riding . . . careless and clumsy . . . making a show of not being overawed by the visitor.*)

JACK   Come on then Hester . . . who's the servant
              round here?

HESTER   We're a bit distracted this morning sir.

JACK   Your front door gaping open . . . street full of
              church officers and all the valuables there for
              the taking.

HESTER   I think we can trust the church officers . . .

JACK   Now that's what I call true faith.

              (*He stares at* RAFE, *slowly recognising him.*)

HESTER   This is Master Rafe Smith, sir . . . the
              haberdasher.

JACK   I know who he is. But he don't remember me,
              do you?

RAFE   Yes. You're Master Jack Lane of Alveston
              Manor.

JACK   Well . . . you knew I was staying here . . . but,
              what I mean is you don't remember me.

RAFE   Have we met?

JACK   You don't remember us swimming in the river
              do you? He don't! I was just a young 'un. Well
              you wouldn't have given me a thought. Now if
              Hester had swum in the river with me, she'd
              remember . . .

HESTER   D'you think so, sir?

JACK   Or Master Smith. If you'd swum with him . . .
              you wouldn't forget that . . .

              (*She glances at* RAFE *and we get a hint of her
              feeling for him.*)

HESTER   Master Smith is a married man!

JACK	God! Swum with him before he was married then.
HESTER	I can't swim.
JACK	If you could!
HESTER	I wouldn't swim in rivers sir . . . you get bitten.
JACK	By what?
HESTER	Six legged things!
JACK	Or two legged?
HESTER	Or fish. They'll nip you and they ain't got no legs . . . 'cept in hell . . .

(She has poured beer for JACK.*)*

Dr Hall won't be long sir . . .

(She exits.)

JACK   And may Bishop Parry bless her from tit to tit. D'you smell that skin as she leans over you? Oh snuffle, snuffle!

(Gets a non-response from RAFE. *Thinks back, puzzled by something* HESTER *said.)*

What'd she mean . . . fish have legs in hell?

(Gives it up.)

You here to see Mistress Hall?

RAFE   Yes.

JACK   Clever Mistress Hall . . .

(RAFE stays silent.)

You tasted her cordials?

(RAFE struggles with his anger.)

She's a sight better at cordials than she is at brewing beer. Good health, and so forth!

RAFE   Good health.

(JACK *takes a good pull and "fights" it down.*)

JACK   I'm here to sit at her husband's feet and see if I want to learn medicine. Go to Cambridge like he did . . . eh? Eh? My father's idea, not mine. Medicine! What is it? Look . . . Dr Hall always insists on having a bowl of watercress put out on his table. Says it's sovereign for the skin. It's in his cure for scurvy. I mean if I become a doctor and I have this lady for a patient . . . do I go up to her and say: "You're looking rough, your ladyship, have some watercress"?

RAFE   His cure for scurvy is very well thought of.

JACK   I'm not saying it don't work. I'm saying life's too short!

(*Sees that* RAFE *is loyal to the doctor and changes tack.*)

Aren't you going to grab these churchmen while they're outside? Money! Hats. Silk trimmings and pearl buttons for the vestments . . .

RAFE   There should be no vestments!

JACK   Ah . . . you a purifier?

RAFE   There's nothing in the Bible that says a man can't lead people in prayer unless he puts a frock on.

(JACK *sees he can bait him.*)

JACK   I remember when we had nothing on at all . . . and you showed us what to do with what we'd got.

(RAFE *knows what's coming.*)

In the river. There were three of us young
'uns. All stark naked in the river. You stood
up out of it and you showed us what it was
about. Water was that cold our danglers were
shrunk the size of catkins. But not yours! Eh?
Yup! You hung a bit of duckweed over it. You
said: as it points to heaven so shall it be
anointed! And you haven't forgotten . . .

(RAFE *slowly smiles.*)

RAFE	Be a liar if I said I had.
JACK	You weren't a purifier then!
RAFE	I wasn't!
JACK	That happened the year King James came to the throne.
RAFE	(*toasts*) King James!
JACK	King James!

(*They drink.*)

Good job he didn't set eyes on it, the bugger!
You'd have been detained at his Majesty's
pleasure!

(*We hear* BISHOP PARRY *leading the way out.*
JACK *makes a show of being solemn.*)

BISHOP	(*off*) And this is where the medicines are prepared?
JOHN	(*off*) Yes, my lord . . .
JACK	Here he comes . . . put on your Sunday face.
BISHOP	(*off*) If I may take a look at your garden before I go . . .

(*The* Bishop *enters through the dispensary into the garden, followed by* John Hall, *his wife* Susanna *and* Barnabus Goche, *Vicar-General of the Worcester Diocese.* Hester *brings up the rear with the Hall's five year old daughter* Elizabeth.)

I understand you grow the herbs that you prescribe here at your own house, Dr Hall . . .

JOHN   Many of them, yes.

(Jack Lane *comes forward and bows low before the* Bishop, *almost insolent in the way he does it.*)

JACK   My lord! Jack Lane of Alveston . . . I think you know my father. He sends his respects and good wishes.

BISHOP   Yes . . . of course . . . I know him well.

(*The* Bishop *manages to disguise his dislike of* Jack's *father.*)

Is he in health?

JACK   Very much so, my lord. Rude health!

BISHOP   And who wouldn't be who lives within five miles of this famous garden. The very scent of it is enough to restore half the diocese.

(*As he moves towards the garden,* Rafe *has to make a decision. He decides he has to bow . . . but very obviously, too late.*)

JOHN   Master Smith, my lord . . . a good friend of ours.

BISHOP   (*a slight edge*) Good morning . . . (*He continues towards the garden.*) So these are the herbs that have the power to save life. To look at them you'd scarcely believe it . . . they seem too beautiful . . . too fragile. I think you're close to God in your herb garden, doctor . . . for where else would you see such a demonstration of his strength than the way he's distilled it into these wisps of flowers and slender stems down to the very roots.

JOHN   I'm very conscious of the hand of God in my work, my lord.

BISHOP I see familiar ones I have at Worcester . . . camomile . . . sage . . . fennel . . . wormwood?

JOHN   Yes . . . wormwood . . .

BISHOP Artemisia absinthium . . . we must be careful with that one. Too much may be harmful, isn't that so?

JOHN   It is, my lord . . . but that underlines the need for accurate measurement of the quantities and the correct balance with other ingredients . . . then it can be extremely beneficial.

BISHOP And, if I recall, you hold that to be the same with bleeding?

JOHN   We should take blood in moderation. Venesection has an honourable place in medicine but the loss of too much blood, by cutting or leeches, can weaken a patient too far. Exact quantity is the soul of good practice.

BISHOP Point me out some of the herbs you might use for a choleric humour . . . red face after meat . . . headaches . . .

JOHN   Well . . . (*Points to herbs.*) Fennel, parsley, butcher's broom, reum officinale, betony, hyssop, rosemary, pennyroyal . . . nettles, not here but in the field . . . and watercress from the brook. And mugwort.

BISHOP All in the one cure?

JOHN	That is one of the basic principles. We use many so that the body can choose those that it needs.
BISHOP	I think my Vicar-General has a question.
GOCHE	Only to continue the theme of God's handiwork . . . how do you react, doctor, to those who hold that sickness may well be visited on us as punishment for our sins and that we should not, therefore, intercede?
JOHN	It's not for me to question God's purpose. What I do know is that he provides me the means of a cure and so intends me to use it. But if he intended to punish, then nothing I could do would prevent that patient suffering.
GOCHE	And then you would turn to prayer?
JOHN	I never "turn to" prayer, sir. Prayer is part of every cure attempt.
GOCHE	Do you always pray with your patients?
JOHN	With those who can, yes.
GOCHE	(*suspicious*) Who can?
JOHN	Those who are not unconscious or speechless with pain. In which case I pray . . . for them as well as myself.
	(*The* BISHOP *is quietly satisfied that the* "*Godly*" GOCHE *has met his match.*)
BISHOP	Mistress Hall, may I borrow your daughter, Elizabeth, to help me bless the garden?
SUSANNA	You do us great honour, my lord. Elizabeth . . . go to him.
	(ELIZABETH *goes to the* BISHOP. *He takes her by the hand and goes to the edge of the herbal bed.*)

BISHOP

Almighty God, we ask thy blessings on this garden. May the fruits of this most benign piece of earth continue to provide thy servants with the means of ministering to the sick and afflicted. And as this child, beside me here, journeys through life may the daily harvest of this soil be life itself. Let it be a place of wholeness and health, where evil shrinks before the divine force of love and goodness . . . In the name of the father, son and holy ghost . . . amen.

(JOHN, RAFE *and* GOCHE *decline to bow the head. Their three "amens" are said clearly and positively. The others murmur, except* JACK LANE, *who mouths it loudly and carelessly in a show of mindless ritual.*)

So, I will leave you as the little keeper of the garden, Elizabeth . . . will you be its keeper for us?

ELIZABETH

I'm too small!

BISHOP

Then you shall grow into the office. But now, I'm afraid we must set out again.

(HESTER *has brought out a phial of honey-coloured liquid, which she hands to* SUSANNA.)

SUSANNA

My lord, my husband has persuaded me to offer you a sample of one of my cordials. I hope you won't be offended . . .

BISHOP

I have heard of your cordials, Mistress Hall and would have been disappointed not to receive one.

SUSANNA

It isn't meant to cure . . . that is my husband's province. A simple recipe to bring ease and well being . . .

JOHN

I can vouch for the ingredients, my lord.

(*Susanna has poured a little cordial into a silver cup. The* Bishop *takes it.*)

BISHOP   An opportune moment . . . as I am about to submit my old bones to a thorough shaking along the way . . .

           (*He drinks.*)

           Hmm . . . not sweet.

SUSANNA   No, my lord. Not sweet.

BISHOP   What do I taste here?

SUSANNA   Vetch flowers and blackthorn sloes with some dried strawberry leaf . . . and something of my own.

BISHOP   Yes. I can feel it doing me good already!

GOCHE   My lord . . .

BISHOP   My Vicar-General says we must go. Which means, of course, that we must go . . . he is the practitioner who mixes the ingredients of my daily round of duties in exact proportions, Dr Hall.

           (HALL *and* GOCHE *exchange cool smiles.*)

           God bless you . . . and you mistress . . . and you Elizabeth and all this present company.

           (JACK LANE *is quick to kneel and shout.*)

JACK   God bless your lordship!

           (*The others echo the sentiment a beat later,* RAFE *in turmoil. The* BISHOP *exits with* GOCHE *who calls through the house to those in the street.*)

GOCHE   His lordship approaches. Make ready!

           (*Cheers from a crowd in the street.*)

VOICE   Stand back! Stand away from the door!

(*All make their way off stage following the*
BISHOP, *except* RAFE *who, annoyed at having
bowed, sits down on the bench, and broods
about it.* JACK LANE *is first to return.*)

JACK   Well that's the show over. Back to watercress.

(*He takes a drink . . . then eats some
watercress.*)

RAFE   I shouldn't have bowed!

JACK   Did I say something? You bowed. Bowing's
what you do, isn't it? Doesn't mean anything.
Doesn't mean you're inferior. Means he's
what he is and you're what you are. (*Thinks.*)
Which is, well . . . (*Unsure, he changes tack.*)
Just ceremony. A bit of ceremony.

(*We hear the* BISHOP'S *party ride away to more
cheers.*)

Away they go. Dr Hall has purged him more
than once . . . and I'll bet you any money his
stools stink like your stools or mine . . . well
maybe not as much as mine . . . Wagh!
Anyway his shit ain't studded with rubies just
because he's a bishop.

(*Re-enter the* HALL FAMILY *and* HESTER.)

JOHN   I never thought he'd stay so long!

SUSANNA   He's grateful to you! If it weren't for you he
wouldn't be alive now.

JACK   That's right, Master Hall. He knows you're
the surest doctor in Warwickshire . . . and
Worcestershire . . . and so do we!

JOHN   I'm not sure that Rafe thinks I should treat
him at all.

RAFE   But I do . . . of course I do! Life is life!

SUSANNA	(*to her husband*) If Rafe has any anti-bishop sentiments, he gets them from you . . .
JOHN	I make it clear . . . and the bishop is well aware . . . that I prefer a church of plain, solid wood, without gilt, paint or glitter . . . but I treat Roman Catholics . . . I'm not a bigot . . . even a Romish priest. In sickness we're all one.
JACK	Seconded!
	(HALL *is a touch pained by* JACK'S *hearty approval*.)
JOHN	Now I must get on with the work. Jack . . . I'm entering the case book. You'd better come and see how it's done.
JACK	Yes doctor.
JOHN	You'll excuse me, Rafe . . .
	(*He leads* JACK *back to the house. Meanwhile,* RAFE, *mastering his feelings, is opening his satchel to show the samples to* HESTER *and* ELIZABETH . . . *in the way he usually does when he calls*.)
HESTER	Oh what excitement! How shall we live quietly now?
RAFE	I've brought the lace and silk . . .
SUSANNA	So soon! (*To* HESTER.) Look at this work!
RAFE	Alice Markham and her mother.
HESTER	You do get things done beautifully, sir! (ELIZABETH *whispers in* HESTER'S *ear*.) Is Bess to have her ribbon?
ELIZABETH	Yes!
SUSANNA	On this day, yes . . . but not every day that Master Smith calls. Choose one . . .
ELIZABETH	This!

(*She points to a ribbon.* RAFE *winds up a length and hands it to her.*)

HESTER	What a lot!
SUSANNA	Not so much! She only needs half a yard.
RAFE	May I make it a gift, mistress?
SUSANNA	No. We can't have you giving your stock away!

(RAFE *is stung.* SUSANNA *softens. She lightens the mood and the inference that he's too inferior to offer her gifts.*)

	We can't have him making himself a pauper, can we Hester?
HESTER	He just wants to give her a little present, mistress.

(HESTER *says it out of her feeling for* RAFE *and* SUSANNA *knows it.*)

SUSANNA	Alright . . . you charge me half a yard . . . and give the rest. (*To* ELIZABETH.) Say thank you Master Smith . . .
ELIZABETH	Thank you, Master Smith.
SUSANNA	Hester . . . you wanted buttons . . . these would do very well, d'you think?
HESTER	They'll do wonderfully, mistress!
SUSANNA	And loops . . .
HESTER	Loops, yes, thank you!
SUSANNA	Now take her up and get her out of that dress.
ELIZABETH	(*protesting*) Oh . . .
SUSANNA	Yes madam. You can't dress for a bishop all day long. Off you go!

(HESTER *is also disappointed to be excluded from* RAFE'S *presence. She and* ELIZABETH *exit.* SUSANNA *appears to examine the contents of the satchel with great concentration.* RAFE *stares at her with equal concentration.*)

SUSANNA   We need buckram selvidge for skirt hems . . .

RAFE   How many skirts?

SUSANNA   Two . . . mine. And one for Elizabeth . . .

RAFE   You should have let me give that gift. I was introduced to the bishop as a friend.

SUSANNA   Well of course you're a friend!

RAFE   I come round myself instead of sending the boy . . .

SUSANNA   Of course!

RAFE   Then don't treat me as a tradesman . . .

SUSANNA   You're in an unkind mood today . . .

RAFE   (*anxious*) No . . .

SUSANNA   Are you punishing me for something?

RAFE   No. You're . . .

             (*He wants to praise her now. She cuts him short.*)

SUSANNA	It wouldn't be right to be always giving gifts from your stock. John wouldn't like it. Suppose he treated all his patients who are friends and asked nothing?
	(*He looks at her as a man in love and she is very conscious of it.*)
	Why are we arguing? You're covered in prickles today, that's what it is.
RAFE	(*smiles*) Not now, I'm not.
	(*She goes back to the buckram.*)
SUSANNA	(*smoothly*) Seven yards. And we'll need thread.
	(*He takes a folding yardstick from its case and measures seven yards of buckram tape. Now it's* SUSANNA'S *turn to watch him.*)
	What was the matter when you met the bishop?
RAFE	What matter?
SUSANNA	What was it about?
RAFE	Bowing!
SUSANNA	Oh why can't those who wish to bow, bow . . . and those who don't wish to, don't. It's like being forbidden to use the sign of the cross. The church won't fall down because of a few gestures.
RAFE	I know, I know . . . but as fast as I think like that my father's shadow falls across me. He'd say no Popery, and that was that.
SUSANNA	We have to be easier on one another . . .
RAFE	I know we do.
SUSANNA	Otherwise we'd have a church of hate . . . not love.

RAFE   I'll save my hate for life!

SUSANNA   (*calmly*) You do not hate life . . .

RAFE   The way I live, I do!

SUSANNA   I'll take this and some of the purple . . .

RAFE   When I compare the way I live . . .

SUSANNA   Don't whip up these storms inside yourself. Be
                calm . . .

RAFE   You know how she treats me!

SUSANNA   If you could be calm with her.

RAFE   She follows me screaming. Wakes me in the
                middle of the night yelling at me . . . I have
                not laid a finger on her . . . but now she calls
                out after me so the street can hear . . . I could
                take her to court and have her charged for it!

SUSANNA   But you wouldn't do that . . .

RAFE   I wouldn't . . .

SUSANNA   You'd open up such a wound it would never
                heal. You must come back to loving her . . .

RAFE   Oh no.

SUSANNA   Then respect her. She's your wife. You should
                respect her . . . as I respect John.

                (*He takes in the implication. She is saying she
                does not love her husband.*)

RAFE   When I compare her with you!

SUSANNA   No. I've said before . . . don't talk like this.

RAFE   You ride among the clouds in heaven where
                she's just the dirt on our shoes!

SUSANNA   (*firm*) Tell me what I've spent.

RAFE   You move about this house like a good angel.
        You have such a wonderful heart and such a
        kind nature. You're what a woman should be.
        They talk about the beauty of this garden.
        Compared to you it's a desert!

        (SUSANNA *moves away towards the house*.)

SUSANNA Leave what I've bought on the bench and tell
        Hester the price. She'll see you're paid . . .

RAFE   I won't come next time. I'll send the boy!

        (*This stops* SUSANNA.)

        I've many a time thought I'd throw all this
        aside and go for a soldier . . . for if it came to
        not exchanging one word with you what would
        anything be worth?

SUSANNA I'm always happy to see you, Rafe . . . and I
        would be even happier if I thought it could
        help you. Don't rage so much inside yourself
        . . . look for the calmness there . . . for it's
        there in all of us. If some things are to be
        endured in life, better to endure with a
        quietness of spirit.

RAFE   You've nothing to endure . . .

SUSANNA Oh? Don't send the boy. We want to see you.
        You're our friend. But, whenever these fits get
        hold of you, think of me telling you to be
        calm. Will you have this picture of me saying,
        "no more storms"? And be at peace . . .

        (SUSANNA *exits.* RAFE *is transfixed and
        anything but at peace*.)

Scene Two

The same, half an hour later. JACK LANE *and* JOHN *enter.* JACK
is being tested.

JOHN	Achillea millefolium?
	(JACK *works at it.*)
JACK	Ha . . . um . . . millefolium . . .
JOHN	Yarrow.
JACK	Yarrow! Yes! I was going to say yarrow.
JOHN	Which parts do we use?
JACK	Flowering stems.
JOHN	How do we administer?
JACK	As an infusion . . .
JOHN	For which conditions?
JACK	The runs . . .
JOHN	Diarrhoea, yes . . .
JACK	Wind . . . backward . . .
JOHN	And?
JACK	The curse . . . the courses . . . women's complaint.
JOHN	Irregular lunar evacuations. Learn the proper terms. You have a list. There's no alternative but to learn it. What would you say of Aconitum Napellus . . . monkshood?
JACK	(*promptly*) Poison.
JOHN	Yes. Name me some poisonous plants.
JACK	Ivy, Deadly Night Shade, Cuckoopint . . .
JOHN	I would prefer you to accompany the names with the Latin. But we'll let it pass for now . . . go on.
JACK	Black-berried briony, thornapple, larkspur . . . except the flowers . . . Christmas rose, henbane, yew . . .

JOHN   Yes . . . you seem to know your poisons . . .

                (HALL'S *tone implies an inordinate interest in this area.* JACK *grins.*)

JACK   That was your first instruction to me, Dr Hall . . . to know what we had to be careful with.

JOHN   I'm well aware of it. You see, when you came to me I thought you might have the usual problem that most have . . . of applying the mind . . . of concentration . . . of absorbing knowledge. But it may not lie exactly there . . . more in your attitude. I have had a complaint.

JACK   (*indignant*) About me? Who from?

JOHN   William Randulph. You sat in the house while I examined his wife and he complains that you looked lewdly at his daughter Agness.

JACK   Who says?

JOHN   His daughter Agness.

JACK   She'd say anything!

JOHN   She did not say anything . . . she said that you looked lewdly at her. Her sister is witness.

JACK   They back one another up, don't they? They want the world to think that men look lewdly at them because it shows they've got something worth looking lewdly at!

JOHN   What happened? Did you look at her?

JACK   Yes . . . I looked.

JOHN   Then you looked lewdly . . . because in my short experience of you, you've never looked at a woman in any other way.

JACK   What should I do? Go about with my eyes shut?

JOHN   To you it's a joke. To me as a medical man it's serious. How will women trust us to make examination of them . . . how will parents trust us with their daughters? Leave the man in you well behind when you become the medical man. Dull your sense of female desirability by sharpening your sense of enquiry. In examining the most womanly of bodies you are simply there to detect the wormcast of disease. (*Pause.*) I'm due to write to your father soon.

(JACK *is instantly on his guard.*)

JACK   But I hope I'll have the chance to put this matter right, doctor.

JOHN   As long as you understand the reason . . .

JACK   No, no. I see the point, doctor . . . I do.

JOHN   I think your father hoped that an exact study like medicine would cool the heat a little.

JACK   I'm foolish about women, doctor. It's a terrible weakness and it's all the worse because I believe I've been given an unfair burden to bear. I don't think any of the men I know suffers it like I do. I can go into a room where there's a young woman like Agness Randulph and no matter how I try to control it she seems in my mind to grow and grow until she fills the whole space and I'm gasping for breath in the corner! I see a sort of shimmer . . . and I sweat . . . and the hairs on my body seem to bristle and raise up!

JOHN   Perhaps we should make you up a prescription. Melissa officinalis . . . lemon balm . . . is good for anxiety disorders. I'll require you to apologise to the family.

(JACK *is relieved that it can be dealt with by a mere form of words.*)

JACK   A man with no guts to apologise is no man at
            all!

JOHN   I'm sure that's true. Do it this afternoon. Now
            . . . to resume. Let's go beyond the plant
            kingdom. Where would we most likely use
            ground coral?

JACK   Fever . . . ungarick fever . . . typhus.

JOHN   How administered?

JACK   Powdered in soup . . .

JOHN   Quantity?

JACK   (thinks hard) Eight drams . . .

JOHN   (aghast) Drams?

JACK   Grains! Grains!

JOHN   You could have given more than thirty times
            the dose. How many grains to the scruple?

JACK   Twenty . . .

JOHN   Scruples to the dram?

JACK   Three.

JOHN   The smallest error could take a life from us
            that could be saved. And every life is worth
            the utmost effort you can make to be exact.

            (HALL crosses to the dispensary and returns
            with a small locked casket.)

            What do we keep here?

JACK   Gold.

            (HALL opens the casket and shows a sheaf of
            gold leaf.)

JOHN   Where would we use it?

JACK   Well gold is universally beneficial. I could use
               more of it . . .

               (*The joke dies.*)

JOHN   Name me a case.

JACK   The same ungarick fever you use coral for.

JOHN   How much coral?

JACK   Eight grains.

               (*He's got it right this time.*)

JOHN   How much gold?

JACK   One leaf.

JOHN   Yes.

               (*He goes to the dispensary and returns with a
               polished chest, the size of a deep pistol case
               and very heavy. He places it on the bench.*)

               And this?

JACK   The lead box.

               (HALL *takes out two sheets of lead from the top
               of the box. They are slightly shaped to the
               profile of the lower back area of a patient and
               have numerous perforations.*)

JOHN   Lead . . . perforated . . . used in this form for
               what?

JACK   That we cannot mention, doctor.

JOHN   Mention it we have to . . .

JACK   The Italian disease. Señor Gonorrhea.

JOHN   And?

               (JACK *thinks.*)

JACK   Strangury . . . ulcer in the bladder . . . women
               with the whites . . . pissing blood . . .

JOHN	How is the lead applied?
JACK	To the reins . . . kidneys . . . so it takes out the heat.
JOHN	And the perforations?
JACK	To let the air through.
JOHN	What is the sign of gonorrhea?
JACK	Yellow puss . . .
JOHN	What potion shall the patient have?
JACK	Venetian terpentine.
JOHN	What else?
JACK	Er . . . erm . . . sasaparilla . . . bark of guaiacum . . . and . . .
JOHN	Yes?
JACK	A lead pipe up your yard for as long as you can stand it.
JOHN	And for females?
JACK	Up the twat . . . oh God, doctor!
	(JACK *feels nauseated . . . but tries to laugh it off.*)
JOHN	Call on God only for the forgiveness of the patient. For in gonorrhea we are treating a sinner. But note . . . we do treat the sinner and we maintain strict secrecy. Now, we've talked mainly of plants and minerals. What I want you to study now are the animal materials we use . . . hartshorn . . . dried cockerel's windpipe . . . earthworms . . . newt and frogspawn waters . . . so that you are able to tell me the appropriate conditions of use, applications and above all, exact quantities. Take my notes and learn the cases.

JACK   Yes! I'll do it, doctor. Don't think I won't. I
                will!

                (HALL *is not convinced.* JACK *has poured beer
                for them both.*)

JOHN   And Jack . . . drink less.

                (JACK *makes a show of pushing the beer
                aside.*)

JACK   Yes! Yes! I'll drink when I'm thirsty and
                that's all. Oh I can do it. I did it once before.
                My father gave me a good allowance and I
                thought this is alright! All I have to do is
                enjoy myself. But now he wants me to work
                my passage through life and sends me to the
                best teacher. I'm lucky. I am lucky. And I'll
                give up the drink . . . the women . . . hunting
                . . . football . . . all of it. Are those things
                worth what I'd have to give up for them?

                (*Enter* HESTER *with a letter.*)

HESTER   Lady Haines's man has just come in from
                Shipston with this, doctor. She's very ill with
                pains in her lower parts and very blown up . . .

JOHN   Let me read what she sends me, Hester . . .

HESTER   Yes doctor . . .

                (HALL *reads carefully.*)

JACK   She's a good old acquaintance of my mother's,
                Lady Haines. (*He hooks two fingers together.*)
                They were like that when they were girls
                apparently. Oh yes!

JOHN   Tell Joseph to saddle Miramont . . .

HESTER   Yes doctor!

                (*She exits swiftly.* JACK *is stung.*)

JACK   And Speedwell? I'll tell her . . .

JOHN	No. I shall go alone. I propose that you stay and catch up on your learning.
JACK	But that's learning . . . seeing a patient.
JOHN	It's going to mean being away at least two days.
JACK	My mother'd be sad if I didn't see Lady Haines . . .
JOHN	She'd be sadder still if you failed in your studies through lack of basic application. Hester!

(HESTER *returns*.)

	We've no apothecary today . . .
HESTER	No . . .
JOHN	Where's my wife?
HESTER	Upstairs doctor . . . having a little sit down.
JOHN	Not well?
HESTER	No, she says it's nothing.
JOHN	Tell her we'll need her services to mix up some prescriptions.
JACK	I'll do that. I'll be apothecary . . .
JOHN	I've said what you are to do . . . (*To* HESTER.) I'll tell her myself . . .

(*He exits into the house.*)

JACK	Well that's fine! Stab me! Keeps me back from seeing the patient. Won't let me make the prescriptions . . . gives the job to his wife!
HESTER	She's done it before, sir . . .
JACK	She's a woman!
HESTER	But she knows what she's doing, sir.

JACK   She's a woman . . .

HESTER   Doesn't stop her knowing what she's doing.

JACK   Don't give me lip . . . she's no business
                meddling in medicine.

HESTER   There's many a time when the doctor's away
                that someone comes to this door saying so-
                and-so in the family's sick and in pain with
                the same complaint they had last week. So she
                gives the same prescription they had last week
                . . . from Dr Hall. He knows she does it. He
                couldn't help but know could he? D'you think
                . . . with someone holding on to dear life in
                terrible agony she's going to say, "I can't
                help. I'm a woman . . . "?

JACK   She's out of order!

HESTER   Don't you criticise her!

                (JACK *is taken off balance by the force of her
                feeling for* SUSANNA. *He changes his tone.*)

JACK   What do I care? I'm to do nothing . . . then
                I'll do nothing as hard as I can. Nihil facere.

HESTER   He said you was to study . . . I heard.

JACK   I'll study you then.

                (*Ogles her.*)

HESTER   You be careful . . . sir.

JACK   Well, what a frosty man your master is! You'd
                think as a doctor, he'd go round spreading
                good cheer. Keep their peckers up. Someone
                you could tell your troubles to. Him? You
                might as well tell them to the north wind.
                What is he but a straight-faced puritan who
                believes he was put into this world to rap its
                knuckles and bring it to order.

HESTER   He never does! Never laid a finger on anyone!

JACK   What? As a church warden . . . reports people
                for coming late . . . or laughing in the sermon.
                That's laying a finger . . . or getting others to
                do it. Reports a fellow for sleeping in the
                belfry with his hat on, on a Sunday. Reports
                the lads who sit in the pews and slide their
                hands in women's placket holes . . .

HESTER   He doesn't!

JACK   You don't think it happens? It's this I mean!

                (*Slides his hand deftly into her placket.*
                HESTER *stands stock still . . . very angry.*)

HESTER   Take it out.

JACK   You can move away if you want it out.

HESTER   I'm not moving sir. It's for you to take it out.

JACK   No, you have to walk away from it, d'you see?
                Otherwise it'll stay there. I'm not master of it.
                I can't tell it what to do . . . and it likes it in
                there. It says, "This is my earthly paradise . . .
                with all the warmth of the world. Soft as silk
                of Araby." It says, "I'll just curl up and go to
                sleepy-weeps . . ."

                (HESTER *can't help smiling. Then jumps away
                as his hand explores.*)

HESTER   Don't!

JACK   That moved you!

                (*Enter* SUSANNA. *She gives no impression of
                having seen. She rapidly checks through the
                ingredients in the dispensary.*)

SUSANNA   Hester . . . we need fumitory . . . germander . . .
                and do we have brooklime?

HESTER   All used.

SUSANNA   Send Joseph, if he's seen to the horse . . .

HESTER   Yes mistress!

                (*She exits quickly.* SUSANNA *begins to pound
                dried herbs in a mortar. She will weigh out
                various powders from containers and mix to
                make up the prescription.*)

JACK   What's he think her Ladyship's got?

SUSANNA   It could be the smallpox . . . or scurvy . . . he
                won't know till he sees her.

                (JACK *is struggling between his pride and the
                need to enlist her help.*)

JACK   Put in a word for me, mistress . . .

SUSANNA   He doesn't want you to go.

JACK   But that's a humiliation. It's a dishonour!

SUSANNA   It's nothing to do with honour. He thinks you
                could use the time better . . .

JACK   Oh mistress . . . you could persuade him.

SUSANNA   Could I? D'you think I don't want you out of
                the house? I'd sooner you went.

JACK   What's that mean?

SUSANNA   I saw what you did to Hester.

JACK   Just a game . . . Mistress Susanna . . . a game.
                We were playing. She laughed.

                (*Re-enter* HESTER.)

SUSANNA   Did you laugh, Hester?

                (HESTER *realises that* SUSANNA *must have seen.*)

HESTER   I told him to take his hand away.

JACK   You smiled! She did . . . she smiled.

SUSANNA   (*to* HESTER) Did you?

(*Now* HESTER *is nervous.*)

HESTER   A bit . . .

JACK   She smiled!

HESTER   Only a bit . . . It's the way he goes on . . . the
                way he won't give up for anything. Well . . . I
                had to smile a bit.

                (SUSANNA *smiles too. She doesn't appear
                severe in any way.*)

SUSANNA   (*to* HESTER) We still have dried germander?

HESTER   Yes by the wall . . .

                (*She gets it and hands the bunch to* SUSANNA.)

SUSANNA   Pick the fumitory, would you?

HESTER   Yes mistress. How much?

SUSANNA   A fair handful.

HESTER   Yes mistress . . .

                (HESTER *exits to the garden.* SUSANNA *carries
                on making the prescription.* JACK *weighs the
                odds.*)

JACK   Well if you want me out of the house . . .
                well . . .

                (*He waits. She goes on with her task.*)

                Persuade him. Only you can . . .

                (HESTER *returns with fresh fumitory. She puts
                it down and is conscious of the confrontation.*)

HESTER   I'll make sure Joseph's gone to the stream . . .

                (*She waits a moment in the silence, then exits.*)

SUSANNA   You already have one apology to make to the
                Randulph's. Make another to Hester.

JACK   To her? She enjoyed it . . . it was a game. You
              don't go apologising for a game. (*Lower tone.*)
              She's a servant . . .

SUSANNA   She's *my* servant.

JACK   Then I apologise to you.

SUSANNA   Well, that would be the easier path . . . but I'd
              sooner you didn't take it. I'm really in your
              hands. My husband will have to know . . .
              There's nothing I keep from him. So I want
              him to know you apologised to her.

JACK   We embraced once. You didn't tell him that . . .

              (SUSANNA *receives this with a cool amusement
              that disconcerts him.*)

SUSANNA   Oh? "Embraced"? That's a strange word for it.

JACK   You kissed me. We kissed!

SUSANNA   As I remember it, you grabbed at me once and
              we wrestled on the stairs . . . and I used my
              elbows. Is that what you mean by "embraced"?

JACK   You kissed me . . .

SUSANNA   Well our heads cracked together. I remember
              that!

JACK   You kissed me!

              (*What started as a piece of opportunistic
              blackmail has turned to desperation that she
              is denying him an amorous moment.*)

SUSANNA   I pushed you away.

JACK   (*desperate now*) You called me "Sweet Jack"
              and kissed me!

SUSANNA   No.

JACK   Oh what is this house? Is it an ice house? Has
              he frozen you? What happened Susanna?

You're only five years older than me . . .
you've been blighted by his damned frost!

(HESTER *re-enters with the brooklime . . . then
hangs back, listening*.)

What happened to you? I remember you at
festival times . . . of all girls you were the one
who laughed . . . or made others laugh. The
time you ran from your father's to the river
singing all the way for a wager with Abbie
Woodward. And you won it! And you danced
. . . you danced like the spirit of the year with
streamers and flowers about you . . . What
happened?

(*However this may trouble* SUSANNA, *she does
not show it. They become aware of* HESTER.)

SUSANNA   Are you going to apologise to Hester?

JACK   Is that what she wants? To see me stoop? To
               see me crawl?

HESTER   I . . .

               (*Enter* JOHN HALL, *dressed for riding with a
               saddlebag. He immediately examines the
               prescriptions*.)

JOHN   Why should you crawl to Hester?

               (*A long pause as he continues to check what
               he needs*.)

               Well? Are our jaws locked? Is no one going to
               speak?

SUSANNA   I think it's for him to tell you.

JACK   (*resigned*) I touched her. Put my hand in her
               placket.

               (JOHN *is unsurprised. Even a little pleased.
               Now he has good reason to rid himself of*
               JACK.)

JOHN   Do we have hartshorn?

SUSANNA   Yes . . .

(SUSANNA *finds him the pot of hartshorn. He could take a piece out and shave it with a small knife, carefully catching the shavings on paper . . . folding it and adding it to the rest, which will be packed in the saddlebag.*)

And the burnt coral?

(SUSANNA *opens a small, polished pot and takes out tiny metal phials, one by one.*)

SUSANNA   Here . . . and pearl, ruby, jacinth and two gold leaves . . .

(*The latter could be placed in the lid of the box and carefully sealed in with a flap.* HALL *adds the box to the contents of the bag.*)

JOHN   Hester, would you bring Elizabeth for me to say goodbye . . . but don't come till I call.

(HESTER *exits to the house.* JOHN *now takes* JACK'S *arm and sits by him.*)

I think it best if my wife stays so that she knows what passes between us in a straightforward manner. I think, first, you should stay home at Alveston the days I'm away.

JACK   But I should be offering Mistress Hall my protection . . .

JOHN   Joseph and his sons are next door at the cottage.

(SUSANNA *almost says something . . . but holds back.*)

While you're home, think about your position. I'll tell you honestly. I don't think medicine suits you . . . no . . . it isn't just the lapses in behaviour . . . though I have to say, if you were in practice it's a weakness that would finish you. And it's not the learning . . . you have a sharp intelligence when you apply it. I think you have an inner contempt for doctoring . . . yes. As a young country gentleman you've lived life at the gallop. And now . . . to have so smirch your hands with the diseases of the low-born, as well as the gentry . . . to show due concern for all . . . and sometimes risk your life for them. To breathe continually the stench of sickness and have to probe into places you'd rather not . . . to examine urine . . . make cures from common weeds . . . scarcely the business of the son of a gentleman! I came from a family not unlike yours and believe me I know to my cost the foregone pleasures. The curb of emotions and easy human fancies bites very hard at first. Unless you're drawn to fighting disease like the hawk to its prey . . . and have no care for anything except that which will cure, then you should stop now and find the right direction for yourself.

JACK   My father'll throw me out!

JOHN   No. I'll speak to him.

JACK   He'll stop my allowance . . .

JOHN   Ah . . . I think not. He'll see the sense of it, I know he will. (*Calls.*) Hester!

(HESTER *enters with* ELIZABETH.)

Here's the pearl I have to leave behind me . . . Come and see me off, Bess . . .

ELIZABETH   Yes father!

(JOHN *picks her up and, as he passes* JACK, *shakes his hand.*)

JOHN

It's for the best, Master Lane. God be your guide. Now. . .

(JOHN *exits with* ELIZABETH, *followed by* SUSANNA *and* HESTER. *As we hear their voices at the other side of the house,* JACK LANE *still tries to think of a way out of the situation.*)

ELIZABETH

(*off*) When will you come home?

JOHN

(*off*) When her Ladyship is well. Pray for her.

SUSANNA

(*off*) Don't have us not knowing. Send word . . .

JOHN

(*off*) I will!

HESTER

(*off*) God's speed, doctor!

JOHN

(*off*) Goodbye!

ALL

(*off*) Goodbye!

(*We hear* HALL *ride away.* JACK *gives it all up and grabs a handful of watercress and eats, angrily.* SUSANNA *returns and after a moment goes into the dispensary to put things back in order.*)

JACK

What's the view like from your tower, Mistress? Oh you look down from your battlements in high old disdain! What do men look like from up there? Like the six wriggly things Neddy Coker sicked up after Dr Hall's amazing emetic? Three grains of mercury vitae and scutter, scutter! And how d'you decide, mistress, which worm comes over your drawbridge and which don't? What I'm saying to you is who do you remember kissing . . . or favouring . . . or fondling . . . or whatever else begins with "f"?

SUSANNA

Why all this outpouring Jack? Why have you taken it into your head to be so offensive to me? You do yourself no justice by it. In all fairness, what have I done?

JACK   You know what you've done!

SUSANNA   He'd have asked you to go in any case. He told
              me.

JACK   I'm not talking about that. I'm talking about
              treachery. You denied me . . .

SUSANNA   I like you. I *do* like you. Yes! But I can't like
              your ways. What would you expect? Jack Lane
              . . . if we were talking about winning a woman
              . . . which we're not . . . but if we were, I'd
              say to you, gently, it's not done by eyeing and
              ogling and pawing in doorways. Or a
              roughhouse on the stairs. It isn't a game.
              We're not the spots on a dice. There has to be
              a wholeness about it. You talk about me being
              frozen . . . look into your own heart, Master
              Playful. Oh you are merry and bright and
              genial with everyone . . . but can you love?
              Are you able to love?

              (JACK *is disturbed by this, then recovers.*)

JACK   Not if I'm denied.

              (*Enter* HESTER *from the house.*)

HESTER   Bess is at Mary Naylor's, mistress . . .

              (*She feels the atmosphere.*)

              Shall I let her stay?

SUSANNA   Yes, that's alright. Hester, would you pack
              Master Lane's belongings for him to go to
              Alveston?

JACK   I'm not going to Alveston. Send them round to
              the Bear. That's where I'll be . . . finding
              good employment for my right arm . . .

              (*Makes motions of downing pints.*)

              You can cross the next three days off the
              almanack . . . 'cos I shan't remember them! If
              he'd have taken me on I'd have given up

drink. Now I'll wade in it! So . . . Hester'll allow a goodbye kiss . . .

(*He grabs* HESTER, *who does allow one kiss . . . but as he gropes she seizes a ladle from a hook on the wall and threatens him . . . half seriously.*)

SUSANNA   You're not taking my advice, Jack Lane!

(*He draws his sword in mock defence.*)

JACK   Have at you! Come one, come all! Mistress, a piece of my advice, in a friendly spirit . . . there's no defence yet devised that don't have some weak point in it. Think back . . . that's what I suggest. Think back . . .

(*He salutes with his sword, and exits.*)

HESTER   I didn't like the sound of that. What did he mean?

SUSANNA   Oh, something very mighty. For a young man he's so full of old sayings.

HESTER   He must have some secret engine somewhere where he churns them out.

SUSANNA   (*works the imaginary engine*) "There's no defence yet devised!"

HESTER   And he fixes you with his eyes when he does one . . .

SUSANNA   (*imitating*) " . . . that don't have some weak point in it!"

HESTER   But you do have to smile mistress . . . you do!

SUSANNA   I know. Give me a hand with the lead box.

(*They pick up the lead box by the handles on either side and carry it into the dispensary.*)

HESTER   So small yet so heavy!

SUSANNA	We need these things back in the right places.
	(HESTER *sorts them out*.)
HESTER	I shall miss his merry voice though . . .
SUSANNA	I don't think the master will.
	(*They laugh at the thought of it*.)
HESTER	Mistress!
SUSANNA	He said I didn't laugh these days.
HESTER	He said what?
SUSANNA	That I don't laugh any more.
HESTER	He says the first thing that comes into his head!
	(*But* HESTER *can't quite disguise the fact that she partly agrees with* JACK LANE.)
SUSANNA	But he's right.
HESTER	You . . . sit . . . more than you used to.
	(SUSANNA *looks as though she might answer this, but doesn't*.)
SUSANNA	Now . . . you'll need to call Bess home and take her to be spoiled by her grandparents . . . You see! This grand visitation has put it out of your head.
HESTER	But you'll be alone.
SUSANNA	Can't help that. They'll be looking forward to seeing her.
HESTER	I thought, with the bishop coming . . .
SUSANNA	They don't know about that. My mother will be sorry to have missed him.
HESTER	But we won't stay the night, mistress.

SUSANNA   You must. They're expecting it. Father does so
                little now. You know how he dotes on the
                sight of her. Whatever light went out in him
                she kindles it again . . .

HESTER   You know the master forgot . . . he thought
                Joseph would be here . . . next door at the
                cottage . . . but he won't. His brother's
                haymaking at Snitterfield. The master said he
                should go . . . he didn't remember!

SUSANNA   Then he should leave his son Tom behind.

HESTER   I'll tell him, shall I?

                (SUSANNA *doesn't want this.*)

SUSANNA   No . . . I'll do it . . . for I wouldn't want you
                late at New Place.

HESTER   You could come with us, mistress!

SUSANNA   Hester . . . have you ever known an hour when
                you could be alone and undisturbed in this
                house? I have to be here. Someone is bound to
                need us. Night is the time when the sick feel
                most helpless. The world goes to sleep around
                them. All they know is they have an ocean of
                darkness to cross to reach the day and fear they
                could drown in their own beds before they get
                there. So someone will send to us. I have to do
                what I can . . . if it's only to get a message to
                John. (*Pause.*) Hester . . .

HESTER   Yes mistress?

SUSANNA   I trust you . . .

HESTER   I'm glad you do, mistress . . . for I've so much
                to thank you for. Where'd I be now if you
                hadn't taken me in? You must know you can
                trust me in anything . . .

SUSANNA   Observe my father while you're there.

HESTER   Has he seen the master?

SUSANNA   He won't admit he's ill. Take careful note of
                how he seems today . . . find an excuse to see
                him in the morning . . . talk to my mother,
                without seeming to pry . . . then tell me
                tomorrow.

                (SUSANNA'S *calm manner still conveys the
                seriousness of her father's state.*)

HESTER   Oh mistress!

SUSANNA   No, no. Not tearful! With a dry eye. As the
                master would say, don't sorrow . . . be exact.
                It's time for me to do something more than just
                sit.

                (*A knock at the street door of the house.*
                HESTER *exits.* SUSANNA *moves to the dispensary
                and checks through the jars there.* HESTER
                returns.)

HESTER   It's little Joe Wardle. His mother's colic's
                come back and do we have the purge?

SUSANNA   Did you say the doctor wasn't here?

HESTER   No. I said I'd see . . .

SUSANNA   Agerick. Senna, rhubarb and cinnamon. Tell
                him to wait. He can take it now.

                (*She measures powders from the named jars.*
                HESTER *returns, her face showing pleasure.*)

HESTER   And now Master Smith is here! At the door . . .

SUSANNA   Ask him to come through!

                (HESTER *calls through the house.*)

HESTER   Master Smith!

(RAFE *enters*.)

RAFE

John passed me on the road and said you might wish to come to supper since you are alone.

SUSANNA

That depends if I'm invited.

RAFE

I'm here to invite you. (*Corrects himself, aware of* HESTER.)

My wife and I invite you . . .

SUSANNA

How kind of her . . .

(*She funnels the powder into a small phial and hands it to* HESTER.)

Hester . . . tell the boy it's as before . . . reduce in three pints of white wine over warm embers for twelve hours, then strained seven times through fine muslin . . .

HESTER

Twelve hours . . . seven times.

(*She exits with the phial.* RAFE *lowers his voice*.)

RAFE

I lied . . .

SUSANNA

Oh?

RAFE

I couldn't invite you home . . . not with her. I couldn't see you at the same table with her. She's not fit to breathe in your presence. But, as luck would have it, I met my cousin, John Palmer . . . I spoke to him just now . . . we're both asked to his house. He wants us both at supper!

SUSANNA

Without your wife?

RAFE

(*hastily*) But with John Palmer's wife . . . Jane . . . well, you know her . . . you know her well, of course you do!

SUSANNA

But your wife won't be there.

RAFE   Don't let that stop you. Dear God! If the
            thought of her prevents you coming, I'll leave
            her. Is my whole life to be nothing? Stone
            walls, narrow streets . . . nothing? Say 'yes'. I
            won't talk like this again. I'm sorry I lied.
            Alright . . . say 'no' and say it quickly.

            (HESTER *returns*.)

SUSANNA   Well you needn't worry about me being on my
            own, Hester. I'm asked to supper at John
            Palmer's . . . with Master and Mistress Smith.

            (RAFE *takes in her "connivance"*.)

RAFE   We'll call for you . . . and walk you there . . .
            at five?

SUSANNA   You see? I shall have company. I shall be safe.

            (*He exits.* HESTER *fights down a feeling of
            jealousy*.)

HESTER   Is Mistress Smith in better spirits then?

SUSANNA   It seems so.

HESTER   Why does she make him suffer?

SUSANNA   She suffers . . .

HESTER   But it's wrong! He's a good man, through and
            through!

SUSANNA   She's had a great loss.

HESTER   His loss too!

SUSANNA   There are some men, Hester, who suffer as
            much from what's inside them as from what's
            happened to them.

            (*But she's aware that his melancholy stems
            from his frustrated love for her*.)

HESTER   What d'you mean?

SUSANNA   No . . . I don't know what I mean. D'you ever
           compare the two of them . . . as men?

HESTER   What? Master Smith with the doctor?

SUSANNA   No! Master Smith with Jack Lane.

HESTER   Oh, but Jack Lane's a hollow man. (*Corrects
           herself.*) Master Lane.

SUSANNA   And which is the proper man?

HESTER   I'm not telling you but he sells ribbons.

           (*They both dwell on* RAFE'S *'properness'.*)

SUSANNA   But aren't we talking of two men who are alike
           in one thing . . . they neither of them really
           know themselves.

HESTER   I don't understand . . . you seem to belittle
           Master Lane. He's kind. He's not thoughtless
           or cruel. You get me to say such things. I'm in
           service here. I'm your servant!

SUSANNA   But much loved, Hester. Much loved. You pity
           him because he's lost both his children.

HESTER   Yes . . . and that he has a wife who blames
           him for it.

SUSANNA   She blames the world. She blames my
           husband . . .

HESTER   But the doctor did everything he could!

SUSANNA   Yes. And they died. And now she can't have
           more. Don't your feelings go out to her as
           well?

HESTER   But not for the pain she causes him.

SUSANNA   She dislikes me . . . yet I feel close to her. For
           I've had no other child in five years since
           Bess was born.

           (HESTER *is well aware.*)

HESTER   Oh mistress!

SUSANNA   You know me . . . you know my greatest fears
              . . . why I sit at the window up there staring at
              the glass. One is that my father may die . . .
              and we'll be helpless to prevent it. And the
              other is that my womb will do the same . . .
              die.

HESTER   No!

SUSANNA   But I have a blessing. I have Bess. She's my
              good fortune . . . and this blackness round my
              heart has nothing to do with her. Get her. It's
              time you were gone. I have some bits of things
              for you to take . . .

              (SUSANNA *exits into the house.* HESTER *is
              overcome by what has passed between them.*)

Scene Three

The same, at night . . . calm and moonlit. Empty.

*Presently, we see the light cast by a lantern in the house,
moving nearer.*

SUSANNA *appears from the house in night dress, her hair let
down. She looks about the garden, holding the lantern high,
wondering why* RAFE *never came.*

*We hear voices far off in the town and a quick snatch of
music on a fiddle.*

VOICES   (*off*) Goodnight! Goodnight! Good friends,
              goodnight! Sleep well! See you tomorrow!

              (*Then silence.* SUSANNA'S *thoughts return to
              her father. She feels she must do something
              for him. She looks for a particular herb — it
              could be plantain — and plucks some. She now
              moves with purpose, going to the dispensary
              and setting up dishes, mortar and pestle.
              There is a small furnace for the burning and*

breaking down of precious stones and
minerals. She opens it . . . the embers still
glow. She places the plantain stems to dry by
it. Then she works the bellows. The fire glows.
She dusts sparks from her night dress, then
takes an old doctor's black gown of her
husband's that hangs there and puts it on. She
takes the box of lead plates and heaves it on
to the bench . . . takes out lead plates and
sprinkles them with vinegar, to ward off
infection. Takes the jar of Venice turpentine
potion and puts it alongside. She opens a
great book, finds the place and reads out loud
in Latin.)

SUSANNA   "Aqua plantago . . . plantago lanceolata . . .
              symphytum officinale . . . veratrum viridis . . ."

              (*These she has in various pots, except the*
              second, the plantain which is drying. She
              assembles pots and comes back to the book.)

              "Curalium . . . incendere . . . (*Thinks,*
              repeats.) curalium . . ."

              (*She puts the book aside and looks in the*
              precious stones pot for coral . . . then realises
              there is none burnt and rendered into powder.
              Again she works the bellows. The fire glows
              very bright, hurting her eyes. She puts on
              smoked glasses of her husband's . . . takes up
              a small crucible, and slipping on a leather
              glove against the heat, she slips a fragment of
              coral into the crucible and holds it in the
              furnace. With her shadow moving on the wall
              behind her as she works concentratedly, she
              looks every inch the alchemist. Suddenly she
              hears a sound from the garden and drops the
              crucible.)

              Who's there? Who are you?

              (RAFE *emerges, having been watching her for*
              some little time. She is not surprised to see
              him . . . but sardonic.)

Rafe?

RAFE   I came over the wall . . .

SUSANNA   Oh? Not out of the moon?

RAFE   I didn't want to bring you to the door. Not so
                late.

SUSANNA   What happened to my supper?

RAFE   (*struggling*) I couldn't . . .

SUSANNA   Is that all I get? "I couldn't"? I won't get fat
                on that. I went hungry for a whole hour
                because of you! Then, when I saw you weren't
                coming I saw to myself . . . . had some bread,
                beef and watercress and got ready for bed.
                Dropped. I have been dropped . . .

RAFE   It was another lie!

SUSANNA   What was?

RAFE   That we were invited to John Palmer's.
                They're not there! They're at their niece's
                wedding in Stowe! The house is empty and
                I'm looking after it . . . I have the key.

SUSANNA   And we'd have gone to an empty house?

RAFE   Yes.

SUSANNA   And had no supper?

RAFE   I meant to go through with it. I meant to take
                you there. But what matters between us is the
                truth. I couldn't tarnish it! Love is the truth.
                And it's the truth because it's the only thing
                of clear, true value. No, no . . . I could rid
                myself of everything else even though I burn
                for it!

SUSANNA   Burn?

RAFE   For that love. Of you. I'd willingly walk into
                the flames.

SUSANNA   You say it as though you'd left God on the
               other side of the wall and stepped into the
               Devil's half acre. Am I a witch?

RAFE   It looked very like it just now. You should
               take care. If you want me to go I can climb the
               wall and no one will ever know.

SUSANNA   I have some honey cakes. Would you like one?

               (*She uses this to get rid of the glove and rope.
               Goes into the house and returns with the cakes
               and a flagon.*)

               There's beer . . . or this wine I was about to
               mix with Venice turpentine for a remedy . . .
               but it's far too good for that. Or I could get
               you a hot nutmeg cordial. That could make
               you happier . . .

RAFE   I'm happy now.

SUSANNA   Eat.

RAFE   Oh to be made of such up and down, see-saw
               stuff that one moment you're in the depths of
               melancholia . . . the next, happy.

SUSANNA   It's because you confessed. You lied. You
               confessed. That's as though you haven't lied
               at all. A great weight lifted from you.

RAFE   Then you confess. You lied. When you told
               Hester you would be going to Palmer's with
               Master . . . and Mistress Smith . . . when you
               knew my wife wouldn't be there!

SUSANNA   But the Palmers are away. We couldn't have
               been going there in any case.

RAFE   What's that to do with it? It doesn't alter the
               lie . . .

SUSANNA   Oh there are lies we all lie that we know won't
               stand up to being breathed on! Within the

hour they're fluttering away like leaves. Not
like lies carved from solid wood from hard oak
that lasts forever . . . that we build our houses
of. Not one of the lies that are always with us.

(RAFE *understands this as a comment on her*
marriage. He makes a decision.)

RAFE   No. I shall go out as I came. No one will
                know. I can't put you in, danger . . . not of
                your soul . . . or our friendship . . . or the trust
                John puts in me. You are the woman I love
                most in the world and he's the man I most
                admire. Look what he's done! Everything that
                makes me so small and shifty and mean-
                minded! He has a calling . . . a cause . . . and
                he sacrifices himself in the name of it. When
                our children were sick he fought endlessly for
                them. He stood up and struggled with death
                himself! And do I pay him like this . . . by
                creeping over his wall in the night to his wife?

SUSANNA   You come to me . . . not his wife. To *me*!

RAFE   I'll take the back ways. No one will see me . . .

SUSANNA   I see you . . . (*She points to the sky.*) Look up
                there . . . a thousand eyes, seeing you!

RAFE   I shouldn't have come in . . .

SUSANNA   But you are in. You're in my garden. My
                husband's by day and mine by night . . . and,
                be warned, you'll not find it easy to leave. Not
                if I conjure you to stay.

RAFE   I'll drag myself to hell but not you with me!

SUSANNA   Is hell so beautiful? This is my night-time
                garden where it's the moon that makes things
                grow. My silver garden with its crop of stars. I
                sit here many a time when he's away and the
                house is asleep. It's then that I'm myself and
                not John's wife. I do secret things. Read his
                books . . . I learn Latin . . . work the furnace

. . . oh yes, as I've watched him do . . . but doing it as Susanna . . . not Mistress Hall.

RAFE   Why have I no strength? I should go . . .

SUSANNA   No . . .

RAFE   You're just taking pity . . .

SUSANNA   I'm not!

RAFE   Or playing with me . . .

SUSANNA   I need you more than you realise. Just as I'm myself . . . and my husband's wife . . . so he is himself, as well as his wife's husband. Five years have made him more himself, less mine. I married a man for a month or two. For the rest, I married medicine. He seemed to have such stature . . . and still does. I respect him, absolutely . . . but in those years, except at the beginning, I don't think . . . I *know* . . . he's never, of himself, reached out and embraced me . . . never really kissed me, by which I mean in pure love. Sometimes we're in the company of a very loving couple . . . well, take the Palmers . . . or Hamnet Sadler and his wife who're my father's age . . . but still he'll touch her hand, or lips, or her ear . . . and she'll open up such a loving smile at him. Well, I've seen a husband and wife leave this house and hug and kiss before they've gone three yards . . . as thought trying to lift some blight they felt when they'd been with us. And when I see that I think my God! What a wilderness I'm in!

RAFE   No. It's a good marriage . . . When you stepped out of Holy Trinity it was seen as the most brilliant marriage of the town . . . the doctor and the poet's daughter! Ask around. Ask them. There's not a person living here who won't say, "this is a good marriage!"

SUSANNA   Oh it's good in other ways, yes. I partly married him out of a fascination for medicine

. . . and that's grown in me more and more, as, you might say, to compensate. In place of love he's let me learn a little of his art. I made my cordials . . . my famous cordials . . . and spent a great deal of time varying the ingredients and noting the results. He knew he had to make some kind of exchange, you see, however unspoken. So it became understood I would use the dispensary when the apothecaries were away. I never troubled him with how much I learned . . . nor ever talked about it with others in case he was criticised. It's been a pact between us . . . never discussed or challenged. Knowledge was there for the picking, as long as I used a small basket and kept it out of sight. But, oh, I wanted that fruit! I've always wanted that which I shouldn't have. Like now. Loving a man who everyone will say she shouldn't love . . .

(RAFE *applies this, as she intends, to himself.*)

RAFE   Loving him?

SUSANNA   Yes.

RAFE   Love?

SUSANNA   Do I amaze you?

RAFE   Love this thing! This pathetic self I drag around with me who dares to think of threatening something he shouldn't even come near! D'you love that?

SUSANNA   No. You.

RAFE   Then you shouldn't. Where love becomes the destroyer, we should all turn from it.

SUSANNA   Love makes . . . not destroys.

RAFE   I only see the downhill road to damnation. From the first time I was invited here I could see you had a powerful bond with him. I've always seen it and blinded myself to it!

SUSANNA	Yes, there's a bond. All who fight disease have it. It's the knowledge that what you fight will always win in the end. You, of all people know how powerless we can be! Oh Rafe! To see children go grey-faced and thin as air! Watch young men wither. Two young girls I'd handled as babies buried by the churchyard elms. There are a hundred sick rooms hereabouts where you might as well say a prayer, shut the door and tiptoe away . . . and one of them I hardly dare enter!

(*She embraces* RAFE *and clings hard.*)

Hold me! Give me some warmth! Hold me!

(*She kisses him. Then begins to undo his clothing.*)

Here. Here in the garden. Then we can truthfully say it wasn't under our roof.

(RAFE *pulls away.*)

RAFE	Now you make me think he's at the door . . . or at the gate . . .
SUSANNA	D'you see which star is on us, high up there? Venus!
RAFE	I see John here . . . sitting with his books. No! There's too much deceit . . .

(*She still points out the star.*)

SUSANNA	"Queen of secrets" Venus, who makes the soldier whisper and the tyrant weep . . .
RAFE	And the honest, dishonest.
SUSANNA	She's there as a sign!
RAFE	Am I honest?
SUSANNA	Look at her . . .

RAFE   Am I what people call honest? Never cheat or
                short change. Keep my promises. I go to
                church. I pay my debts. I don't deny my
                mistakes. I admit it if I'm in the wrong.
                Mostly . . . mostly, I do . . . even now I'm
                saying I can fall short of the mark . . . well . . .
                that's honest. So is caring for your wife when
                she hates you. Trying to be a good father when
                I was a father . . . isn't all this what defines
                an honest man? Yes? So how can the same
                man still think himself honest when he cheats
                in love?

SUSANNA   Because he's not the same man! Love changes
                us. Love's alchemy! In that furnace everything
                changes. Hard stone shatters, iron goes soft
                and turns to liquid. They change their colours
                and their kind and become something other
                than themselves when they're in the fire . . .
                and so do we . . . in love's fire!

                (*She takes his hand and puts it to her breast.
                Now he no longer resists and kisses her,
                pulling her night dress to her waist as they
                kneel among the herbs . . . she taking off his
                shirt . . . then, out of the passion, a moment of
                calm.*)

RAFE   I've been in the dark so long! So many empty
                nights I've stood by that wall . . . looking at
                your window . . . trying to draw you out to me.

                (*Suddenly* SUSANNA *puts her hand to his
                mouth. She's heard something. They listen.*)

SUSANNA   There's someone in the house. (*Listens.*) In
                the hall. (*Listens.*) By the stairs.

                (RAFE *tries to get into his shirt.* SUSANNA *pulls
                up her night dress. Both freeze as they hear*
                HESTER'S *voice.*)

HESTER   (*off*) Mistress!

SUSANNA   Hester!

(SUSANNA *gets the old cloak and buttons it round her.* RAFE *gathers up his things and exits the way he came, over the wall.* HESTER *enters. She sees* RAFE *departing. Then sees* SUSANNA.)

HESTER   Mistress . . . I could hardly see you . . .

(*She is clearly shocked by what she's seen.* SUSANNA *is angry.*)

SUSANNA   Where's Elizabeth?

HESTER   With your mother, mistress . . .

SUSANNA   Why aren't you with her? I said come tomorrow! Why are you here?

HESTER   Your mother begged me to come . . . though I was frightened to . . .

SUSANNA   (*half guessing*) Why?

HESTER   Because of your father . . .

SUSANNA   He's sick?

HESTER   Yes mistress. Oh he's very ill. So much so I cried for an hour. That's all I came to say.

SUSANNA   (*low, as though to her father*) Did I stop thinking of you for one moment! (*To* HESTER.) I'll dress . . .

(*She makes a move then feels she must explain.*)

We've not long since come from supper . . . at John Palmer's. Master Smith came back to see that I was safe . . .

(HESTER *doesn't believe her.*)

HESTER   Yes mistress.

(SUSANNA *becomes aware of someone else in the hall.*)

SUSANNA   Who's with you?

HESTER   It's Master Lane . . . he saw me walking and
            insisted he walked with me . . . I couldn't say
            "no".

            (JACK LANE *emerges from the shadows,
            obviously having been listening. He's been
            drinking.*)

JACK   How are you Mistress Hall? How's the warden
            of the castle? Has the drawbridge been down?

            (HESTER *makes to go but* SUSANNA *stops her.*)

SUSANNA   Have you and he been together?

HESTER   No mistress!

JACK   I escorted her through these streets lady.
            You'd be surprised, there's all kinds of men
            creeping about tonight whose purposes
            wouldn't bear too much scrutiny . . . I'll be
            glad to take you to your father's . . .

SUSANNA   You're not fit to go anywhere!

JACK   Oh yes I'm fit. Most fit. I'm back to being
            myself again . . . and as a true and expert
            graduate of the tap room I'd say I was at least
            two quarts away from losing company with my
            legs. But I will have one of your dainty little
            cakes for ballast . . .

            (*Eats one.*)

SUSANNA   I've no time for you now. I'd be glad if you'd
            leave.

            (*But* JACK *is staring into the dispensary.*)

JACK

Hey ho . . . now . . . look here! You been making up a prescription madam?

SUSANNA

Something for myself . . . now go.

JACK

Don't say that . . . not that! Tell your mistress to be more careful Hester. I can see what's set up there. Venice turpentine potion. A Venetian remedy for an Italian complaint you get when Cupid's arrows turn rusty. Well he was an Italian himself, Cupid, wasn't he? And he's certainly been doing his work here. Sarsaparilla . . . guaiacum bark . . . and I can see the lead plates got out. Those tell-tale lead plates for the nameless condition. What else would they be for?

(*As* SUSANNA *and* HESTER *react to this, a slow fade.*)

END OF ACT ONE

ACT TWO

The garden, two days later. Glorious sun. SUSANNA *and*
ELIZABETH *wear wide-brimmed straw hats as they gather herbs
in baskets.* JOHN, *just returned from his journey, sits writing
up his notes.*

In the dispensary everything has been tidied away. SUSANNA
stands and points across the garden.

SUSANNA   Get me eyebright. Two stems . . . and three of
               St John's Wort.

               (ELIZABETH *runs to a spot in the garden to pick
               the herbs.*)

               The white flowers and the yellow. Do you
               know them?

ELIZABETH   Yes!

               (*She returns with the two bunches.*)

SUSANNA   Eyebright to bathe the eyes and St John's Wort
               for a healing ointment. Long ago the Knights
               of St John bound their wounds with it and if
               you hold the leaves to the light you can see the
               tiny wounds in them . . . poor leaves . . .

ELIZABETH   Poor leaves!

SUSANNA   Which is herbigrass?

               (*She holds out her basket to* ELIZABETH *who
               chooses one.*)

               Yes. Some call it rue . . . but I like herbigrass
               because it means the Herb of Grace. You can
               use it as a charm to keep away the Devil . . .

               (*For a moment she thinks back to* RAFE *in the
               garden. Then quickly she hugs her daughter.*)

               What would he do if he came in and saw it?

ELIZABETH   He'd run!

JOHN   (*looking up from his work*) Lady Haines has
                been blessed by the Lord with the most
                undefeated sprit! There she sat. Bolt upright,
                even in her illness, in a bed almost as wide as
                the Earl of Northampton's . . . and the canopy
                over it as high as that walnut tree . . .

                (*He indicates offstage.* ELIZABETH *marvels.*)

SUSANNA   (*to* ELIZABETH) Ask him what colour . . .

ELIZABETH   What colour?

JOHN   What colour . . . hmm . . .

SUSANNA   There's a question . . .

JOHN   But do I have the answer? Yes . . . blue and
                gold . . . with gold velvet curtains and a
                tapestry on the wall of a boar hunt . . . not my
                taste and a rather unquiet companion for the
                bedchamber I thought . . . she's a splendid
                lady, very forthright and vigorous . . . but she
                was in some pain in the stomach and felt that
                little ants were biting her all over . . .

ELIZABETH   Ants?

JOHN   Not real ants. (*To* SUSANNA.) A common
                enough symptom of scurvy.

SUSANNA   You think you'll have to return?

JOHN   Possibly not. As scorbutic fevers go the heat in
                her was not as great as it can be . . . she
                seemed well on the way to recovery this
                morning. They'll send if they have to . . . but
                if she has the jelly of hartshorn in her broth
                and the herbs every day, it should clear. Now
                you ladies . . . will you leave me out here to
                complete the case book. I must do it while it's
                fresh in the mind.

SUSANNA   (*to* ELIZABETH) Tell Hester to bring the doctor
                his liquorice drink.

ELIZABETH   Yes, mother!

(ELIZABETH *exits.*)

JOHN   It's been so warm!

SUSANNA   We've had no proper rain for eight days.
              We're bringing water from the river.

              (JOHN *smiles with pleasure at the garden and
              takes* SUSANNA *lightly by the wrist.*)

JOHN   God is good to me.

              (*At once he lets her hand go and turns from
              her. The surprise of the small gesture makes
              her feel momentarily guilty. But she quickly
              recovers.*)

SUSANNA   I wanted to talk to you about my father . . .

JOHN   His breathing. Is it worse?

SUSANNA   No . . . he still takes the pomegranate oil. I
              made up some more . . .

              (JOHN *gives her a slightly cooler glance.*)

JOHN   Did you?

SUSANNA   It's done him so much good. But now there's
              something else . . .

JOHN   What?

SUSANNA   I'm not sure . . . a fever of some kind that
              comes and goes . . . he won't talk to me about
              it in case I tell you . . . and he won't let
              mother send for you. I tried to get Hester to
              question him while she was there but he
              realised right away . . .

JOHN   I'll find some excuse to talk to him.

SUSANNA   He used to be so strong . . .

JOHN   Don't worry. We'll devise a plan.

              (*He smiles at her. Again she feels a quick
              sense of guilt.* HESTER *enters with a tray.*)

SUSANNA   (*going*) When you've finished, Hester . . .

HESTER   Yes mistress . . .

                (SUSANNA *exits as* HESTER *pours the drink and
                also places a letter for him which he's not
                immediately aware of.*)

JOHN   So the bees didn't swarm?

HESTER   No sir. What we need is some thunder to get
                them stirring.

                (*She exits.* JOHN *sips the drink and open his
                case book. He takes a pen and starts to write.
                Only now does he notice the letter. He opens
                it and reads. The contents shock him. He
                thinks about it, carefully.*)

JOHN   (*calling*) Hester! (*Pause.*) Hester!

                (HESTER *re-enters.*)

HESTER   Yes doctor?

JOHN   When did this arrive?

HESTER   Just now sir . . . young Yarwood brought it
                from Master Whatcott.

JOHN   Bring the wax.

                (*She senses an atmosphere.*)

HESTER   Yes sir.

                (*She exits.* JOHN *takes a sheet of paper from
                his writing stand and starts to write, breaking
                off to control his emotions . . . then resuming.*
                HESTER *returns with the wax and lighted
                candle, cupped in her hand.*)

JOHN   Just a moment . . .

                (*He finishes writing and, sanding the letter,
                folds it so it can't be read.* HESTER *puts the*

candle to the wax to let a blob fall on the letter.)

And again.

(HESTER *is aware that he's being extra careful with the contents of the letter. He presses his ring to the wax.*)

It needs to go right away. Take it yourself. It's only a minute or two . . .

HESTER	Master Whatcott's?
JOHN	No. (*He writes the name.*) To Master Smith.

(HESTER *is pulled up by this. She senses trouble.*)

HESTER	Yes doctor.

(*Now* SUSANNA *enters, looking for* HESTER.)

SUSANNA	Hester . . .
JOHN	She's taking a letter for me . . . not far.

(*He nods to* HESTER.)

HESTER	Yes sir.

(*She exits.* SUSANNA *suddenly thinks of something.*)

SUSANNA	That's not to my father?
JOHN	No . . .

(*Again, to her surprise, he takes her hand and, this time, quickly kisses it.*)

I sent a note to Rafe Smith.

SUSANNA	(*outwardly calm*) Why?
JOHN	I've asked him to come and see us . . . because of this letter. It's from your father's old friend, Robert Whatcott. I'll read it out to you

. . . but I won't ask anything . . . or comment.
It's going to shock you. But it's for you to
dismiss what's in it!

(*He takes the letter.* SUSANNA, *hiding her
fears, sits to listen.*)

(*reads*) "Dear Cousin. My affairs have called
me away from Stratford until tomorrow but I
felt I should send you this with no more delay,
since it deeply concerns Mistress Susanna and
yourself. I was at the Bear with a party of
acquaintances last night and encountered
Master Lane. He was, I might say, for him,
only a little impaired by drink. He saw fit,
there and then, before this company, to
slander Mistress Susanna. I will not convey
his innuendo and gestures . . . but specifically
what he said. He told us that she suffers from
a venereal disease . . . the running of the
reins . . ."

(*He looks at* SUSANNA *for her reaction. She has
a strange look . . . as though almost
anticipating this. She answers distantly.*)

SUSANNA   The running of the reins is gonorrhea . . .

JOHN   He's a foul-mouthed slanderer and that's now
               we must treat him!

               (SUSANNA *thinks back to* JACK LANE'S *last
               visit.*)

SUSANNA   He's saying I have gonorrhea?

JOHN   It's the implication of it he wants. It doesn't
               matter to him that it's impossible for you to
               have it . . . no question of it . . . no symptoms
               of it . . .

SUSANNA   I? I have no disease whatsoever!

JOHN   I know you haven't.

SUSANNA   It's revenge.

JOHN   Of course it is! And that's how we must view
              the second of his slanders . . .

SUSANNA   Another?

JOHN   Yes . . . and worse than the first! He's the son
              of a good father . . . from a family that must
              be horrified that he sinks to this. He's a
              blundering fool but I wouldn't have taken him
              as evil! (*Reads.*) "He added to this that he had
              certain information that Mistress Hall had
              been naughty with Rafe Smith . . . by which he
              meant they had known one another . . . and
              that this took place at the house of his cousin,
              John Palmer, the house being empty these last
              four days and the key left with Master
              Smith . . ."

              (*He looks to her, inwardly desperate for a
              denial. SUSANNA is quietly composed.*)

SUSANNA   I have not been at John Palmer's.

              (*JOHN is visibly relieved.*)

JOHN   Dear God, grant us strength of mind and
              clearness of purpose!

SUSANNA   The last time I was at John Palmer's you were
              with me . . . What was it? A year ago?

JOHN   Yes. Oh this has no sense about it! It's
              vindictiveness! (*Reads.*) "We had hot words
              with Jack Lane but he would not retract,
              though Robin Foster, one of our party, came to
              blows with him. I was very angry that so
              virtuous a woman as your wife should be so
              traduced." He says he's more than willing to
              act as witness to confirm the slander. I can
              speak with him tomorrow.

              (*He crosses to her and kisses her on the head,
              putting the letter in her hands.*)

I'm to blame. I shouldn't have expected Jack
Lane to behave any way but badly. I should
have spoken with his father first and made
sure he went back to Alveston. He's punishing
me through you . . .

SUSANNA   But making me feel I'm the cause of it!

(JOHN, *treading carefully, is wary of this.*)

JOHN   How?

SUSANNA   By using my name. It's there! It's because I
asked him to apologise to Hester!

(JOHN *is relieved. If she is in any way the
cause, he would rather she didn't say but hold
to a total denial.*)

JOHN   He must retract. He must openly retract in
public and admit he invented these stories out
of spite. And he must apologise to you . . . and
to Rafe . . .

(*He looks at her carefully.* SUSANNA *is
composed.*)

SUSANNA   Poor Rafe . . . to have your friend dragged into
this . . .

(JOHN *notes the use of "your".*)

JOHN   As I rode out to Shipston, I met him in the
street and, hearing you were to be alone he
offered that you should go to supper with him
and his wife.

SUSANNA   No . . . that didn't happen.

JOHN   But he said he'd come round to invite you . . .

SUSANNA   Yes, he did that. But later he had to return
and say that *she* didn't feel up to it.

(HESTER *enters. She is nervous about their
close conversation.*)

HESTER   I'm sorry doctor . . .

JOHN   Did you deliver the note?

HESTER   Yes sir.

JOHN   Did he say he'd come?

HESTER   He said nothing sir. Nothing . . . and getting
              back here Master Morton was at the door. He
              has this lump on his neck, sir . . .

JOHN   He's here himself . . . in person?

HESTER   Said he couldn't wait doctor. You're to either
              cure him or kill him.

JOHN   Anyone with him?

HESTER   His son, I think. A big lad.

JOHN   You saw the lump?

HESTER   Here. (*Points to her neck.*) Size of a duck egg.

JOHN   I'll give him a poultice so his son can take
              him home. Hester, go to the sacking in the
              corner where the worms are. Fetch me three or
              four . . . alive . . .

              (HESTER *winces and exits to garden.*)

              (*to* SUSANNA) So . . . you don't have any
              disease . . . you haven't been to John
              Palmer's . . . and you haven't seen Rafe
              Smith . . .

SUSANNA   Yes I did. I told you. I saw him twice . . .

JOHN   I mean . . . not on any other occasion . . .
              alone.

              (SUSANNA *is quite firm.*)

SUSANNA   No. Never.

JOHN   I'll see Master Morton . . . then we'll decide
              what's to be done.

(HESTER *returns with a dirty piece of linen containing the worms. She hands them to* JOHN.)

HESTER   Four.

JOHN   Thank you.

(*He glances quickly at them, then exits to house.*)

HESTER   (*turning to* SUSANNA) I've heard what's been said, mistress. I've heard from Robin Foster's sister, Ellen. Robin was there when it was said!

SUSANNA   I want you to help me . . .

HESTER   Does the doctor know he was here?

(HESTER, *driven by her feelings for* RAFE, *is quite fierce.* SUSANNA'S *reply takes her aback.*)

SUSANNA   Yes. I told him. But I did lie to you about something, Hester, and I want to put the matter right . . . you were present when he came to invite me to supper with him and his wife at John Palmer's. You heard him?

HESTER   Yes. But not all . . . I didn't hear all.

SUSANNA   Well that's why he came . . . and that's what he said. But then, later, he had to come back to tell me his wife didn't want to.

HESTER   But it was night time!

SUSANNA   He'd walked the streets for hours, not daring to come and say.

HESTER   Why did he run and get over the wall when I came?

SUSANNA   He didn't want me to he embarrassed by him being here and for that same reason I told you a lie. I said that we had just been to supper at

John Palmer's . . . I'd not been at John
Palmer's. I had not been away from the house.

HESTER   Yes, I thought that was strange . . .

(*She means she thought it strange because she
assumed that she'd been with* RAFE *at the
house. As it comes into her mind it brings her
close to tears.*)

You took him! And damn you for it!

(SUSANNA *doesn't want any of this to be heard
from the house. She speaks firmly and
quietly.*)

SUSANNA   Don't damn me, Hester. Don't damn me. I did
not "take" him. He came here, himself, for the
reason I said . . .

HESTER   Are you going to dismiss me?

SUSANNA   No . . . I've told you before . . . you are much
loved.

(*A kind of recklessness, out of frustration, has
got hold of* HESTER.)

HESTER   Do you love him?

SUSANNA   As I love you.

HESTER   Do you love the doctor?

SUSANNA   I deeply respect my husband, Hester.

HESTER   If I had a husband I'd love him . . .

(SUSANNA *is getting tired of this.*)

SUSANNA   Well, you can't have Rafe Smith!

HESTER   Neither can you!

(HESTER *finds herself laughing at her own
defiance.* SUSANNA *laughs at the shock of the
reply.*)

Now you'll get rid of me!

SUSANNA   No . . . I want you to help me. I never went to
           John Palmer's and you didn't see Rafe
           climbing the wall. You understand? You can
           simply say, if you're asked, that he left before
           Jack Lane came into the garden. He could have
           left by the side gate.

HESTER   But mistress . . . don't you think Jack Lane
           saw him climb the wall?

SUSANNA   No . . . no, I don't. For, if he saw him here,
           he'd have said it happened here . . . not at
           Palmer's.

HESTER   That's true.

SUSANNA   Help me through this and I'll make more of a
           sister of you than a servant . . . we'll live in
           friendship here . . . in this house and this
           garden . . . enjoying our life. We'll set aside a
           marriage portion for you . . . and I'll do my
           best to help you find a good husband . . .
           someone less complicated . . .

           (*They have to smile.*)

           Less stormtost . . .

           (*They laugh.*)

HESTER   Yet how can he be that? He was the light of
           my life.

SUSANNA   Hester . . . what fools we can be!

           (HESTER *reads in this an admission that she
           did "take" him. A knocking at the door.*)

HESTER   Oh mistress. I must answer that.

SUSANNA   Help me?

HESTER   Yes . . .

SUSANNA   You know what has to be said . . . and not
               said?

HESTER   I know.

               (*She exits.* SUSANNA *moves to where she and*
               RAFE *embraced. She stares at the ground,*
               thinking hard. HESTER *returns hurriedly.*)

HESTER   Mistress . . . it's Master Lane!

SUSANNA   Tell my husband.

HESTER   I have mistress. He's still with Master Morton.

SUSANNA   Then tell Jack Lane I want him to go and not
               come within a mile of this house!

HESTER   He's weeping, mistress.

SUSANNA   He's what?

HESTER   Weeping.

               (JACK LANE *enters and falls to his knees.*)

JACK   Mistress Hall! Hear me now, for I've fallen so
               very low I fear I'll never raise my head again
               among those that count as anything in this
               world. I know you've had the letter . . . Robert
               Whatcott's letter . . . no, listen mistress!

               (SUSANNA *makes as if to leave.*)

SUSANNA   If you're going to retract, do it. There's only
               that I'll listen to . . .

JACK   I'm ready to do it, lady . . . why else am I
               here? It's what I swore I'd do when I woke up
               this morning blank as a sheet of paper and
               they told me what I'd done.

SUSANNA   (*to* HESTER) Bess is still over at the cottage. Go
               to her and keep her there awhile.

HESTER   Yes, mistress . . .

SUSANNA   And remember . . .

(*She and* HESTER *recall their talk.*)

HESTER   Yes mistress . . .

(HESTER *exits.*)

JACK   All we have to do is to find the form of words.

SUSANNA   Words?

JACK   Yes . . . you know . . . "words". Those things
            we speak freely and lawyers charge money for.
            Well words are words . . . they mean this then
            that . . . they won't stand still. They run
            around like ferrets . . .

SUSANNA   You slandered me deliberately!

JACK   There you see . . . "deliberately". There's a
            word . . .

SUSANNA   Maliciously and deliberately.

JACK   Malicious? No! Me to you? No! Deliberately? I
            wouldn't! I would not . . . *did* not. And that's
            all I'm saying, we have to find a form of
            words for . . . to cover a queer old situation
            where I retract . . . totally . . . that which I do
            not remember uttering.

(*Enter* JOHN HALL *from the house.*)

JOHN   I should have left orders for you to be barred
            from my house . . . though I never expected
            you to show yourself here. You realise this
            slander has reached everyone . . . here's my
            patient, Master Morton has heard them
            already!

JACK   And I'm sorry for it, doctor . . . I'm sorry for
            it. But it wasn't me doing it deliberate. My
            tongue got out and did the talking . . . that's
            the size of it. It's like when you have to
            apologise for your dog getting loose and biting
            someone. My tongue's my dog, that's what it
            amounts to.

SUSANNA   He says he will retract but doesn't remember
                 what he said.

JACK   I don't, doctor . . . I don't!

JOHN   Are you telling us that Robert Whatcott lied
                 about it?

JACK   No. Not Bob! No! He's the straightest man I
                 know . . . and I've known him four years . . .
                 played quoits and nine pins with him. Never
                 go against the truth Bob wouldn't . . . so what
                 he said in the letter is the bona fide of it . . .
                 but I can't say if it was or wasn't.

JOHN   Why?

JACK   For the usual reason doctor, and I'm not proud
                 of it. What with the shock I'd had here and
                 finding myself floating footloose . . . I took a
                 bit too much on board. I know I said I
                 wouldn't drink but that was in another set of
                 whatever . . .

SUSANNA   But Robert Whatcott, you say, is a truthful
                 man?

JACK   Not casting anything against Whatcott. Not
                 anything.

SUSANNA   He says that when you made this slander you
                 were not drunk.

JACK   Me? Not drunk?

                 (JOHN *appreciates his wife's shrewdness.*)

JOHN   In his opinion you were not impaired by drink.

                 (JACK *is only thrown for a moment.*)

JACK   Well . . . his opinion! He could have seen it
                 like that! He could indeed have done so . . .
                 for I hold it well. And that's not me saying
                 that . . . others say that. But that's only the

outside of a man. In here . . . (*Points to his
head.*) was a very different picture. I may have
been upstanding but my mind was laid out,
embalmed and ready for the last rites . . .

SUSANNA   You remember that, do you?

JACK   Yes . . . I remember the general, broadscale,
               mistress . . . but the particular I don't. The
               exact, as the doctor would say.

JOHN   Jack . . . it just isn't credible that you fail to
               remember two very specific slanders: that my
               wife has gonorrhea . . .

               (JACK *fends off the thought of it.*)

JACK   Oh doctor! . . .

JOHN   And has had carnal knowledge of a man you
               name . . . at a place you name. These are
               exact! So exact that no one would be believed
               if he said he'd forgotten them.

SUSANNA   They were lies, Jack Lane! It's no use you
               trying to claim that they must have just
               slipped out . . . as though you're saying, "well,
               it's true really but I have to say sorry".

               (JACK *wants her out of the way.*)

JACK   This is so painful for Mistress Hall, doctor.
               Let you and I decide the form of words and
               bring it to her . . .

SUSANNA   No. I'm the one you aimed this at! I wish to
               hear all that's said.

               (JOHN *also might have liked it to be settled
               between the two men. He takes pen and paper
               and makes notes as he speaks.*)

JOHN   You should avow publicly that you now realise
               you committed slander . . . that the statements
               you made were entirely false . . . That you
               withdraw those statements unreservedly and

that you apologise for the distress caused to
Mistress Hall . . . and to Master Smith.

(JACK *weighs it. Beams at them.*)

JACK   That's good doctor! That's good! That helps
          me. "I *now* realise I committed . . .", which
          leaves aside whether I remember or not . . . or
          was impaired or not. Yes!

          (JOHN *has passed the paper to* SUSANNA *who
          considers it carefully.*)

SUSANNA   But this is like saying you didn't realise at the
          time but do now. You knew all along what you
          were doing.

          (JOHN *has been looking for the easier way but
          has to agree.*)

JOHN   Then it must be. "I agree I committed
          slander."

JACK   "I agree that I committed slander" . . . yes,
          well . . . yes. That's good too. I'll have that.
          And stronger for you, mistress, which is only
          right . . .

SUSANNA   We should agree that the retraction is written
          as well as spoken so nothing gets changed.

JACK   Good . . . right . . . yes.

JOHN   Then I propose that the written retraction be
          posted up in the porch of Holy Trinity Church
          and that the spoken is made there next
          Sunday. I'll speak to his reverence . . .

JACK   In church? I wasn't thinking in church for it!

JOHN   God has been listening to every word we've
          said. And God was listening when you said the
          words you said. It seems to me appropriate you
          should retract them in God's house.

JACK   If they'd been said in church, yes. But this
                happened in the Bear . . . and what I thought
                was that I would retract those words in the
                Bear in front of those same gentlemen who
                were present last night.

JOHN   It's gone far beyond them! The whole parish
                knows . . .

JACK   And the whole parish will know that I've
                retracted if it's at the Bear. The written notice
                can be posted up on the door. The landlord'll
                do that for us, I promise. I don't think
                Mistress Hall wants it dragged through Holy
                Trinity.

                (JOHN *thinks him too eager to settle and is
                suspicious.* SUSANNA *doesn't want the chance
                of a quick settlement being lost.*)

SUSANNA   Do it! As long as it's done and done
                thoroughly. Is there any more to say?

JACK   Well yes . . . that's an agreement I make with
                you. The question is what agreement you
                might make with me.

JOHN   This man! You can't be asking me to reinstate
                you here!

JACK   No sir. Not that. No . . . no . . . not
                reinstatement . . . no. Not that. That's not on!
                Not in the same house, no. But you asked me
                to consider carefully what calling I wished to
                follow. Well, I have . . . and it's still
                medicine. It's only when it looked like I'd lose
                it that it came to me how much I wanted it.
                There's a doctor near Leamington called
                Harper. D'you know him?

JOHN   I know him, yes.

                (JOHN's *reply carries disapproval.* JACK *picks
                it up.*)

JACK   Oh he's not like you, doctor. More my style,
                you could say. Likes his comforts. Likes a
                laugh. I think he'd take me on if you
                commended me . . . and you could persuade
                my father it was a good move . . . that I'd paid
                for my mistake and you bore no grudge . . .

                *(They see he's fishing to keep his allowance
                and has been all along. Both are full of anger
                but held back by their desire to settle.
                Suddenly HESTER enters from the garden.)*

HESTER   Doctor!

SUSANNA   Bess?

HESTER   It's not her, mistress . . . she's safe at the
                cottage. No . . . it's Master Smith . . . he came
                round to us and asked if Master Lane was with
                you. I said he was. He stayed for a while . . .
                in a terrible state, doctor. I saw him coming
                over and came to warn you.

JOHN   He's not here.

                *(Enter RAFE from the garden, distraught,
                dishevelled.)*

RAFE   Yes he is!

JACK   Rafe! We've talked. I take it all back. I shall
                publicly retract. We've agreed and that's an
                end to it.

                *(RAFE suddenly rushes to him and gives him a
                blow that knocks him to the ground.)*

RAFE   That's to make sure it is!

                (JACK gets up slowly, mustering his dignity.)

HESTER   No!

JOHN   In God's name!

SUSANNA   He's agreed they're lies! The stories are false!

JACK	(*to* RAFE) Oh you were so big in the river! You think you're as big on dry land? You think I'll let myself be dusted up by a twopenny haberdasher . . . (*Draws his sword.*) You're going to need some dash . . . I'd dash now if I were you . . .
JOHN	Sheathe it! Don't add more!
JACK	What you doing doctor . . . protecting him? Anyone does that to a gentleman knows what's what. His light goes out!

(RAFE *suddenly takes hold of his doublet and holds it high in one hand. It puzzles* JACK *and the others. It's as though* RAFE *is holding it high like a weapon or standard. Then he whirls the jacket round* JACK'S *sword and charges him again to the ground, disarming him. He takes the sword and throws it high offstage.*)

RAFE	Your sword's in the dirt. Follow it.
JACK	I don't stir till you put it back in my hand.
JOHN	Rafe! Come to your senses! Hester . . . find the sword and bring it back.

(HESTER *exits to the side gate.*)

This must be kept in bounds. I see enough wounds and hurts that I can't prevent without seeing them inflicted in front of me. Oh God take anger from our hearts and let us come together in understanding.

(HESTER *returns with the sword.*)

Give it to me.

(*She does so. He holds the pommel to* JACK.)

There is no dishonour in forbearance.

(JACK *takes the sword and puts it back in the scabbard.*)

Rafe? You hear?

(RAFE *puts on his doublet.* SUSANNA *is now alarmed that a settlement is in danger. She must prevent* RAFE *confessing . . . as he may be about to do.*)

SUSANNA   We're close to an agreement. He's ready to declare that the statements were untrue . . . that there is no substance to them!

JACK   No substance? No substance, mistress? "Substance"! There's another word. What d'you call substance? I came round here the night before last to see Hester through the streets from your father's . . . you were in the garden here in the dark. I overheard you say to Hester that Master Smith had seen you home from John Palmer's house where you'd been to supper. Next morning I heard that the Palmers were away at Stowe . . . at their niece's wedding . . . and that they always leave the key with Master Smith. Substance? Substance? I came out here and saw Mistress Hall wearing your cloak, doctor . . . and a lamp lit in the dispensary. I saw things interfered with, like she's always doing while you're away. I said what was she prescribing and she says "something" for herself. Venice turpentine potion on the bench. The lead plates out of the box and on the bench. For herself? I saw it! Substance? Oh I have substance . . . and I was prepared to let it go but not now! What I said I'll say again and anyone who cares to come round to the Bear can hear me. And if that puts me on the road to hell, doctor, it's a road that started right here at your house!

(*He exits.* RAFE *makes to follow.*)

RAFE   I'll head him off!

JOHN   Rafe, please! Force will make matters worse.

(RAFE *turns to him as a despairing penitent. He still thinks that* JOHN *must know the truth about him and* SUSANNA.)

RAFE What must I do? Say what you wish me to do?

(JOHN *suspects what this means but pretends not to. All the same, his glance at his wife gives his thoughts away. For once,* SUSANNA *reveals her own inner strain.*)

SUSANNA Jack Lane has nothing! (*She regains her control.*) Hester . . . Master Lane says that he heard me tell you the night before last that Master Smith had seen me home from supper at John Palmer's. Did I say that to you?

HESTER I remember nothing like that, mistress . . . no.

SUSANNA Master Smith was just leaving, wasn't he?

HESTER Yes mistress.

(RAFE *realises that* HESTER *saw him.*)

By the side gate.

SUSANNA And Master Smith was here to tell me supper was cancelled.

HESTER Yes mistress.

(RAFE *now realises that a story has been put together and that* JOHN *may not know about their liaison.*)

SUSANNA (*to* HESTER) What was I wearing when you came back?

(HESTER *hesitates.*)

Oh Hester. You can tell the doctor I was wearing his old gown. He knows I wear it in the dispensary so nothing splashes on me. Would I have just come from supper wearing it?

*(She realises that she may be protesting a
little too much.)*

I could see there was work to do in there and I
spent an hour putting things in order and
wiping the jars and phials with vinegar
against infection . . . it hadn't been done for
some time. I took the lead plates from the box
to sprinkle them, leaving them out on the
bench. Master Lane saw them and
misunderstood.

(JOHN, reluctantly, has to probe this a little.)

JOHN   He said you told him you were making up
            something for yourself.

SUSANNA   Yes. I did make up something earlier . . . a
            tonic from meadowsweet.

            *(Under SUSANNA's gaze RAFE feels too
            intimidated to confess openly. But he still has
            the urge to do so.)*

RAFE   John . . . forgive me!

            (JOHN carefully 'misunderstands' him.)

JOHN   I'm sure our Heavenly Father forgives you.
            You may have acted in anger . . . but you
            struck down what you saw as evil.

RAFE   *(puzzled at first)* No . . . I don't mean that . . .

            (SUSANNA heads him off.)

SUSANNA   I think we should discuss now what we mean
            to do . . .

            *(But JOHN's desire is to defuse the situation.
            He knows his wife will talk RAFE out of
            confession if they are left alone.)*

JOHN   Yes. Hester . . . find young Tom and tell him
            to be ready to deliver a letter to the vicarage at
            Holy Trinity.

HESTER	Yes doctor.
	(HESTER *exits across the garden to the croft.*)
JOHN	The only course now is to charge him with slander . . . defamation, and defamation is for the church courts, not the civil courts. You don't have to see him now if you'd rather not. You need to come with me, Rafe.
RAFE	Me?
JOHN	You are also defamed . . . by implication. You're named.
	(*He lets the implication of this sink home.* SUSANNA *is anxious to prevent* RAFE *being questioned if she can.*)
SUSANNA	There's still another way, surely. Let me talk to Jack Lane.
RAFE	No!
	(*He pulls himself up, realizing he has answered for* JOHN. *The latter treats it calmly.*)
JOHN	What would you intend to do?
SUSANNA	If I talk to him alone so that he has no audience to play to . . . and no confrontation.
	(*She glances at* RAFE.)
JOHN	I'd be happier if you didn't. I don't want it said that you coaxed him into agreement. And, really, what understanding could be reached? He'll always want more . . . and if he gains an advantage out of it that'll only serve to make people suspicious. He is the guilty party . . . you the innocent. It's for the guilty to 'deal' and wrangle. Innocence must take the straightest path.
RAFE	But we'll be questioned!

JOHN   Of course . . . and we'll need to give answers
                that are unwavering and unconfused. If we
                decide to do that, then it only remains to
                consider whether we can stand up to the pain
                of seeing it through.

RAFE   John!

JOHN   No . . . consider. Don't make a hasty
                judgement. I have a book of Ecclesiastical law
                in the house. I'll see if it can help.

                (*He takes his portable desk and exits to the
                house. We can sense that he has left them
                alone deliberately.*)

RAFE   They must know!

SUSANNA   They don't. No one does.

RAFE   Hester?

SUSANNA   Yes . . . she saw you climb the wall . . . but
                she won't say so.

RAFE   But wasn't Jack Lane with her?

SUSANNA   He stayed at the street door. He didn't come
                out into the garden till you'd gone. He didn't
                see you. So nothing needs to be said!

RAFE   But it does!

SUSANNA   Nobody saw . . .

RAFE   Hester saw me! Are we to put on that girl the
                burden of telling a lie as she did just now?

SUSANNA   She would do anything for you. We'd make a
                nightmare for her if we forced her to harm you
                by saying what she saw.

RAFE   She won't have to if we confess . . .

SUSANNA   Ah! "Confess"! I knew that word wasn't far
                off! Rafe are you here to comfort your

conscience or to remember the words of love
you spoke? We pledged our love. That is no
sin. He said love one another . . .

RAFE   He said do not covet your neighbour's wife!

SUSANNA   Covet? We don't covet . . . we love! Hate is
              the sin . . . not love!

RAFE   We are condemned if we don't confess . . .

SUSANNA   We're destroyed if we do!

RAFE   I can't be disloyal to John . . .

SUSANNA   But you can to us? This is bright day . . .
              remember the night . . .

RAFE   I remember shadows that change everything.

SUSANNA   Yes! We were in Love's Kingdom that has it's
              own state . . . it's own laws . . . and, once
              there, we were other than we are now. I said!
              We have two natures . . . and God gives us
              both of them. God has more worlds than we
              can imagine. We build a church and
              lightening strikes it down. His plagues carry
              off the holy with the sinner! How can we know
              him or his purpose?

RAFE   What we did was unlawful . . .

SUSANNA   Not to God! Why create that in us if it were
              not to be used?

RAFE   You can't make a stream run uphill . . . you
              can't change right and wrong . . .

SUSANNA   And what was wrong? What was unlawful?
              What did we do? They'll talk of carnal
              knowledge. Did we have that?

RAFE   Carnal means flesh. I touched your naked
              body . . .

SUSANNA   You know what they'll want to know. Was it
              consummated? That's what they hang on.

That's what brings the saliva to their mouths!
Did you enter me? No! So we can truthfully
say "no".

(RAFE *thinks he hears someone. He makes a
gesture then continues.*)

RAFE   I dread him overhearing when I haven't had
the courage to tell him. And you? How can
you leave him in ignorance? He's talking of
the consistory courts . . . talking to Parson
Rogers. You can't let him go into that not
knowing . . .

SUSANNA   He knows already.

RAFE   How?

SUSANNA   He's guessed.

RAFE   Are you certain?

SUSANNA   It's in his look . . . his tone. It's in everything
he doesn't say.

RAFE   Then I must talk to him now!

SUSANNA   No! That's the last thing he wants. He knows
and mustn't know. He wants our silence.

RAFE   That's a travesty of him and you know it. He's
the most honest man I know.

SUSANNA   Honesty is not one thing! Love is not one
thing . . . nor loyalty . . . he is loyal to his
practice and his patients. He's honest in that.
And that is his love. And I come second . . .
which I accept . . . oh yes! I've seen the terror
in the faces of the sick . . . how they reach out
to him, their only hope. I can't put myself
before that and don't expect him to. So . . . he
wants our silence because, if we speak, all that
would be shattered like glass . . . Lady Haines
would shun him, Lady Rainsford and
Underhill . . . the Earl of Northampton . . .
and the rest . . .

RAFE   (*deprecating*) So . . . he'd lose their fees . . .

SUSANNA   We need the fees of the better off so he can
                treat the poor.

RAFE   And for this he condones what we did?

SUSANNA   Not condones. Doesn't want it said.

RAFE   But I've gone to church with him. I've prayed
                with him. . . I've watched him pray and
                wished I had the purity he has. He should be
                coming at us with a flaming sword! I can't
                believe that, even in the case of his practice,
                he would put anything before God himself!

SUSANNA   That depends what you mean by God himself.
                If God himself wants the sick to die in pain. If
                God himself wants plagues and pestilence. If
                God himself tears children from their parents
                with their lives unlived . . . as yours were . . .
                was that God himself?

                (*She expects anger. But* RAFE *becomes
                calmer.*)

RAFE   You have no right to put my children in the
                scale against what we know we should do . . .

SUSANNA   Why? Why should we?

RAFE   Because I honour him!

SUSANNA   How can you honour him by destroying his
                work?

                (*He knows he must agree. She takes in his
                change of heart.*)

                It's only a matter of what you leave out. You
                came back to tell me that supper was
                cancelled. I was working in the dispensary. It
                took a few minutes to tell me. Hester arrived
                as you were going.

RAFE   But if he asks me directly if we've known one
                another?

SUSANNA   He won't. And, in any case, we haven't . . . in
                the sense it would be meant.

RAFE   (*sad that it has to be said*) No . . . no.

                (RAFE *puts his head in his hands. She pities
                him.*)

SUSANNA   If it were left to me I'd leave it. Let it drop.
                Soon forgotten. Women are slandered every
                day . . . they're slandered by the hour! Not so
                much spoken . . . I could walk through
                Stratford market and be called a whore fifty
                times over . . . not in words . . . in looks . . .
                in sneers and nudges. You put on armour
                against it as a girl and try to wear it lightly.
                I'm sure worse things have been said. But we
                must fight it . . . not for ourselves . . . not
                even for him . . . but for those he might save.

                (*As she looks across the garden she sees*
                ELIZABETH *at the cottage.*)

                There's Bess . . . playing in the grass. (*She
                waves to her.*) What a long road we travel . . .

                (JOHN *enters with his law book.*)

JOHN   Have you considered?

SUSANNA   Yes.

JOHN   And you're resolved?

SUSANNA   Yes.

JOHN   You're ready to go through with it in court?
                Rafe?

RAFE   Yes.

JOHN   You will both affirm that you were never alone
                together . . . at John Palmer's . . . while I was
                away or at any other time?

RAFE   Yes! Yes!

JOHN   And you Rafe, like Susanna, have never had
            any symptoms of the disease . . . and will
            swear to it.

RAFE   I don't have to swear to that!

JOHN   (*carefully*) Lane is implying that it passed to
            her from you. You have to deny it . . .

RAFE   Of course I deny it!

JOHN   And you vow that you are both entirely
            innocent of the charge . . .

SUSANNA   Yes.

            (RAFE *does not answer, but nods instead. We
            sense* JOHN'S *relief. He 'covers' it by applying
            himself to the book.*)

JOHN   It seems that in a case of defamation, where a
            married woman is slandered, she is able to
            bring the charge herself . . . in her own name.
            Also, the case would not be heard at parish
            level but at the diocesan court at Worcester
            Cathedral.

            (RAFE *is shaken by this.*)

RAFE   You mean the bishop's court . . . *in* the
            cathedral?

JOHN   Yes. The consistory court of Worcester.
            Though I doubt if the bishop will appear. He
            delegates the running of the court to his
            Vicar-General.

SUSANNA   He was here with him . . .

            (JOHN *recalls the dislike he formed of* GOCHE.)

JOHN   Yes.

RAFE   But he's a puritan!

JOHN   It's what I'm frequently called, Rafe . . . and
                I've heard people hang the label round your
                neck for some of your reformist views. What
                you mean is he'll be strict and have a mind to
                the dignity and discipline of the church courts
                . . . and that I approve. We needn't fear it.

RAFE   He isn't even in Holy Orders.

JOHN   He represents the bishop. He will apply the
                letter of the law.

RAFE   I've heard he was forced on the bishop by
                those who want someone to crack the whip.
                That the bishop never would have appointed
                him otherwise . . .

JOHN   Gossip!

RAFE   I saw his face . . . here, in this garden, when
                you put him down!

JOHN   I did not 'put him down'.

RAFE   John! Over the treatment of the sick when it
                might be a visitation from God!

JOHN   I simply spoke what I thought.

RAFE   Oh, he'll question us!

JOHN   Then we'll give clear and positive answers . . .

RAFE   I mean he'll question us hard!

JOHN   (*becoming impatient*) Then we must face it
                hard!

                (*Enter* HESTER *from the house.*)

HESTER   His reverence says he's willing to talk right
                away, doctor.

JOHN   Thank you, Hester . . . these slanders of
                Master Lane's . . . we shall be taking him to
                court at Worcester and we'll need you as a
                witness . . .

SUSANNA   Not Hester, surely . . .

JOHN   To say what she heard and didn't hear the
              night before last. It's evidence.

HESTER   You mean . . . to go with you and say it in
              court, doctor?

JOHN   Yes . . . and to swear it on oath.

              (HESTER *has exchanged a look with* SUSANNA.)

HESTER   But what if it's only something I don't
              remember hearing?

JOHN   Then that's what you swear to. It's quite
              simple. You swear that you don't remember.

              (*Again* HESTER *appeals with a look at* SUSANNA.
              SUSANNA *looks away*.)

HESTER   Yes doctor . . .

              (*She hesitates a moment, then exits to the
              house*.)

SUSANNA   There is a way, of course, of avoiding
              questions . . . of having no testimony or
              swearing and having the whole case dealt with
              in a matter of minutes. I mean, if Jack Lane
              pleaded guilty.

              (RAFE *weighs this*.)

RAFE   He'd never do it . . .

SUSANNA   His greatest fear is that his father will cut him
              off . . . leave him in what he would call
              poverty. Yet all the time he can't stop himself
              behaving in the way that would bring it about.
              Half of him defies his father . . . half is on its
              knees! If he fights this case and loses . . .

JOHN   As he will!

(He gives them both a look that defies them to doubt it. They owe him loyalty.)

SUSANNA   I'm not talking of guilt or innocence but winning or losing a case. If he loses he'll shame his family . . . he'll have to do public penance . . . and his father may well cast him out. But if he pleads guilty and shows contrition, the penance will probably be in private . . . to a chaplain, say . . . and his family will be spared a good deal of distress. And so his father could afford to be more lenient.

RAFE   And there'd be no case!

SUSANNA   A case, yes . . . but not one to be argued.

RAFE   Would we have to appear?

SUSANNA   Appear, yes . . .

(She looks to her husband for confirmation . . . but he doesn't respond. She detects that his self-imposed patience with them is wearing thin as they reach for the easiest solution.)

RAFE   But we simply hear him plead . . . and be sentenced . . . then come home?

SUSANNA   I believe so, yes.

(JOHN struggles to control his sudden distaste.)

JOHN   You want me to persuade the father to persuade the son . . .

RAFE   Think what we'd avoid!

(JOHN's frustration speaks out.)

JOHN   I know what we'd avoid! We'd avoid what we all three of us avoid . . . and avoid . . . and avoid!

(RAFE, half expecting it, matches him.)

RAFE   Then let's not do so! Let's face it now!

JOHN   And why not now? Yes now!

RAFE   It's all I want . . .

JOHN   Then praise God!

RAFE   Amen!

SUSANNA   No . . . this is foolish! Stop there! (*To* RAFE.)
                    This is not what you want. (*To* JOHN.) Nor is it
                    what you want . . . nor what I want . . . and we
                    know it. What shall we do? See this clearly?
                    Or wallow in self-accusation? If we believe
                    God wishes the sick to be healed then we must
                    believe that he singles out those who can
                    master the art of healing them! You are such a
                    man. He has set you on a path that you are not
                    free to leave . . . and that we must help you
                    follow or fall from grace!

JOHN   Yes! The path of sharp stones for me, the
                    primrose path for you!

SUSANNA   No! Keep our peace! Calm ourselves. Keep our
                    peace . . .

                    (RAFE *behaves as though controlled by her. A
                    silence.*)

RAFE   Let me speak . . .

SUSANNA   Don't break it. Keep our peace . . .

                    (*Again, a silence.* JOHN *moves through the
                    garden.*)

JOHN   D'you see this June day? This bright June day
                    . . . how the air shimmers, brimming with
                    God-given warmth . . . and the flowers fill
                    with nectar? But I've seen another picture . . .
                    I've seen the wall broken down on three sides
                    . . . the house roofless . . . the garden open to
                    the winds . . . stark, staring winter howling

through . . . and all this abundance withered
into dead stalks.

(*He turns to them.*)

Then help me. I'll do as you say . . . write to
his father . . . persuade him. But whatever
happens . . . whether we get a plea of guilty or
not . . . I want you both totally decided to go
with me every step and never break faith.
We'll go to that court, cathedral or no . . . and
we will not be overawed or dismayed. We will
present our own case . . . with no advocate . . .
since innocence needs no advocate. And when
the case is won, as it must be . . . I daren't say
Please God . . . I daren't say it! But when
they've closed the book on it and it's won and
we come home . . . then we'll begin from there
. . . anew. And all that needs forgiving . . . in
any of us . . . must be forgiven . . . and seeing
us forgive, our Heavenly Father may find it in
his heart to have a little mercy on us . . .

(*He has taken the attitude of prayer.* RAFE
prays with him full of fear.)

RAFE   Maker of heaven and earth have mercy!

(SUSANNA *prays, relieved that a confession
from* RAFE *has been avoided once more.*)

SUSANNA   And thy blessings, Lord, be on us from this
time forth . . .

(*The bells of Worcester Cathedral begin to
ring in great clashing disharmony. As they
remain in prayer, we either see the garden
almost blown away, and replaced by cathedral
. . . or it is done in blackout.*)

Scene Two

Worcester Cathedral. *An alcove near the western end of the
south aisle where the consistory court is held.* RAFE *and* JOHN
still stand in prayer. SUSANNA *is kneeling. Their heads are*

*bowed. Around them the echoing sounds of the daily traffic of
the cathedral.*

HESTER *enters quickly, but pauses, uncertain whether to
interrupt. She has a letter. Presently* SUSANNA *looks up and
sees her.*

SUSANNA   Hester?

HESTER   Yes, from Master Lane's father! Peter Diggory
                brought it . . . (*She hands over the letter to*
                JOHN *with a smile that betrays the contents.*)
                He rode two horses from Alveston and got to
                Worcester in under two hours!

RAFE   Why did he wait so long? Why wait till the
                day of the trial?

                (JOHN *still hesitates to open the letter.*)

JOHN   You've told no one about this?

HESTER   No . . . and told Peter to tell no one.

JOHN   No one saw it arrive?

HESTER   No . . . I watched at the gate of the inn yard
                and stopped him as he galloped up . . .

                (*Now* JOHN *opens the letter.*)

JOHN   Yes . . . Lane says: "My son is of my mind and
                will plead guilty. I think he shows much
                courage to make this confession and that, I
                hope, stores up some credit for him . . ."

RAFE   All that torment! Our thanks, dear Lord, for
                this deliverance!

JOHN   (*suddenly bitter*) Yes . . . you thank him!

SUSANNA   As we should. All good things proceed from
                God.

                (*She moves away to pray silently.* JOHN *moves
                to her.*)

JOHN   I didn't tell you . . . I put a postscript in my
            letter. I said if we got this agreement I'd do
            my best to help his son.

SUSANNA   Then that was well said.

JOHN   It is a sin!

SUSANNA   Generosity to an opponent?

JOHN   It's only generosity after the event. To offer it
            before is bribery.

            (*She sees* RAFE *looking troubled by their
            whispered conversation.*)

SUSANNA   It was nothing more than a general offer of
            help. (*Prays.*) For this blessing bestowed upon
            us, Oh Lord, we truly thank thee.

            (HESTER, *who has been gazing up at the
            vaulted ceiling of the nave suddenly sways
            and gives a little cry.*)

JOHN   What's this?

SUSANNA   She must have run here, all the way.

HESTER   No, no, mistress. I was looking up. I've never
            seen anything so high. I was afraid it would
            fall.

JOHN   And fall it may . . . if we don't uphold it.

            (BISHOP PARRY *enters.*)

BISHOP   Dr Hall! I was told of your arrival just now.
            And Mistress Hall . . . I'm deeply shocked that
            Lane should have brought such charges after
            the consideration and hospitality you bestowed
            him. Master Smith! You show great strength
            of character to here!

            (RAFE *is at first pleased, then worried by this.
            The* BISHOP *has been given a hint about* RAFE
            and SUSANNA *but, like them, conspires to bury
            it. He corrects course slightly.*)

Slander must always be confronted. I'm
pleased to see you bring the case so promptly
. . . and in my court . . . and all three of you
standing here together . . . I was going to say
to proclaim your innocence . . . but I'm always
reminded that I must not comment on any
specific case . . . not in my untutored way. My
Vicar-General has the legal training. I must
leave it to him.

(*A slight, awkward pause.*)

And how is my little keeper of the garden?

SUSANNA   Very well, my lord . . . and with her
                grandparents.

BISHOP   Who may well have a certain fondness for her?

SUSANNA   I think they have, my lord.

BISHOP   Your cordial worked on me wonderfully well,
                Mistress Hall. I can quite see why you're so
                celebrated for them. That day I actually
                covered five miles without suffering my usual
                aches and agues . . . and the Malvern Hills
                looked even more like a portion of paradise set
                down on earth.

                (*A moment as the* BISHOP *tries to think of
                another topic.*)

                I think back with great pleasure to that visit,
                doctor. I was reminded of our conversation
                about the letting of blood when a physician
                from Bristol was here recently . . . Edward
                Chalmers . . .

JOHN   I've not met him . . .

BISHOP   He was interested in your view, and asked
                whether it may have been the result of your
                studies at Montpelier in France. A doctor of
                Lyon wrote against excessive venesection . . .
                isn't that so?

(JOHN *is respectful but terse*.)

JOHN   Yes . . . a well argued case. But my
            conclusions are drawn from my practical
            observations, my lord.

BISHOP   At Montpelier?

JOHN   In Stratford, my lord. I like to test everything
            against experience.

            (*Enter* GOCHE, *the Vicar-General. He greets
            the* BISHOP *and bows slightly to the others*.)

GOCHE   My lord! (*To the others*.) Good morning. With
            your lordship's permission . . . Mistress Hall
            . . . you the case of Hall versus Lane?

SUSANNA   I do.

GOCHE   Then I have to tell you that, it being past the
            hour of the convening of the court . . . and
            there being no other cases to hear this
            forenoon . . . I have, accordingly, dismissed
            the case and dispersed the court for this time.

SUSANNA   I thought we had to appear . . .

GOCHE   You've not heard?

            (*She shakes her head slightly. He looks at the
            others.* RAFE, *inwardly jubilant, leaps in*.)

RAFE   That he's decided to plead guilty, yes . . .

            (*An uneasy moment.* GOCHE *is interested in
            this unexpected response.* RAFE *realises he
            shouldn't have spoken*.)

GOCHE   Ah! That is your information, is it? Master
            Smith?

RAFE   (*more cautious*) I may have misunderstood.

GOCHE   Were you aware of it?

(*He looks keenly at* SUSANNA *but* JOHN, *impatient already with* GOCHE'S *inquisitorial manner, answers for her.*)

JOHN   We were, Master Goche. We all were. I had it from his father by letter just now.

GOCHE   I see. And that was what your lordship was discussing when I came?

(*The* BISHOP *is somewhat intimidated by* GOCHE'S *manner . . . but can, on this, answer firmly.*)

BISHOP   No. Because I was *un*aware. I had not heard of it.

GOCHE   (*to* JOHN) You had not imparted this information to his lordship?

(*The* BISHOP *has a distaste for this line of questioning.*)

BISHOP   The matter did not arise, since I had made it clear that I would hear nothing concerning the case. I deduct from this that what has actually happened is nothing so positive as a plea of guilty . . . ?

GOCHE   The plaintiff has committed the act of contumacy . . . Master Lane has decided not to appear.

JOHN   How? How can he decide that?

GOCHE   By not turning up, Master Hall. He's not even in Worcester. He's still in Stratford-upon-Avon. The companion who was to ride with him came on alone. He said Lane had a back injury and couldn't mount a horse. But a cleric who had stayed in Stratford a few days and came here this morning said he'd seen him out riding in Sheep Street at six. A carrier who came later tells us Lane was drinking ale and brandy all night and

claiming that this court has no jurisdiction
over gentlemen of his station.

JOHN   What will happen to him?

BISHOP   You sound concerned, doctor.

JOHN   Yes . . . to my surprise I am, my lord. He was
              my charge . . . and I hate to see a young man
              so injure himself with his pride.

GOCHE   The sentence for contumacy is
              excommunication.

              (JOHN *and the others are visibly shaken.*)

BISHOP   This will be the lesser of the two forms of
              excommunication; that is to say, the offender
              is excluded from divine service and receiving
              the sacrament. He will not be denied the
              company of all Christians . . . which is
              reserved for such acts as heresy.

              (GOCHE *produces a folder containing the
              document, together with ink and quill.*)

              In former times I would have had the bell
              tolled as for a funeral . . . closed my book and
              put out a candle. But we are now reformed.
              We send a letter to be read out at his church
              before the congregation.

              (*He signs.*)

GOCHE   Indeed, my lord, there are too many absenting
              themselves and not caring whether we
              excommunicate them or not!

JOHN   The Lane family will care deeply, my lord.
              They are devout Christians and regular
              churchgoers.

GOCHE   Of the old school, Dr Hall? Gentry Christians
              with their own pew and velvet cushions and,
              no doubt, believing there is one law for them
              and another for the rest! They thumb their

noses at this court . . . Oh we'll soon hear
their lofty protests when we sentence him to
do regular public penance instead of money
quietly changing hands. No . . . we will not
sentence him in absentia as they would wish
but insist he presents himself here to this
court, or, my lord, we must take out a writ of
excommunicato capiendo and have the civil
authority commit him to prison!

(*The* BISHOP *is nervous of the zealot factions
who support* GOCHE. *He treads carefully.*)

BISHOP   Step by step, Master Goche. We'll discuss it
later . . . but for now Mistress Hall you've won
your case. The plaintiff has show himself
guilty of his actions. Congratulations! I will
see it conveyed to Stratford that there is not
the slightest stain on your character . . . or
yours, Master Smith. Well, I am called away
. . . but I hope you will remain to see the
wonders of this house . . .

GOCHE   (*swiftly*) My lord . . . since the parties have
come so far and have not even been able to
present their case, I think I owe it to them to
discuss it informally . . .

(*A moment as the* BISHOP *realises all too well
what* GOCHE *intends.*)

BISHOP   Of course . . . if that is their wish. God bring
you safely home and may the light of the Lord
guide your feet to the paths of righteousness.
In the name of the Father and of the Son and
of the Holy Ghost . . . amen.

ALL   Amen.

(*The* BISHOP *exits.*)

JOHN   We shall need to make ready for the road, your
reverence.

GOCHE   Of course doctor. We'll be brief. I think you'll
                   still have more than enough time to arrive by
                   sunset. I have some papers relating to the
                   evidence. One moment . . .

                   (GOCHE *exits*.)

SUSANNA   He means to question us . . .

RAFE   But we can go. The bishop said it's our
                   choice. I can see what he intends!

JOHN   And how would that look? He's offered to
                   discuss the case. I can't see how we can
                   refuse.

SUSANNA   At least let Hester go!

JOHN   She's a witness.

RAFE   But it's over! The case is dismissed!

SUSANNA   We'll tell him we need her to prepare us for
                   the journey. Hester, go to the inn, quickly . . .

HESTER   Yes mistress.

                   (HESTER *wants to go but feels the doctor's
                   disapproval.*)

                   When shall I say we're leaving, doctor?

JOHN   (*reluctant*) In half an hour.

RAFE   I'll go with her!

JOHN   No! You have to stay.

RAFE   Say I have matters to attend to before we start
                   out. That the girth strap of my saddle is being
                   mended and I have to see if the work's done!

                   (*He stops making excuses and becomes
                   defiant.*)

                   Tell him I will not be questioned!

JOHN   Rafe . . . let Hester go . . .

(HESTER *exits.* RAFE *is devastated.* JOHN *resigns himself to the truth coming out.*)

Whatever you have to say to him you must say. I can't ask you to put your immortal souls in danger . . .

RAFE We could have been safe!

SUSANNA We should tell him what we intended to tell the court. And that alone. Just as we decided. Nothing is changed. Nothing!

(*Re-enter* GOCHE *with a dossier of papers.*)

GOCHE It's high time for young men like Master Lane to realise that the days of the lawless gentry are over. There's nothing these spoiled, loutish loudmouths like better than to come from their country estates and throw their weight about in town. Oh yes, we've known a good deal about Master Lane for some time . . . (*Taps the documents.*) Complaints stick to him like flies to honey. Yet why are so many ready to report him? He's good humoured, genial, free with his father's money . . .

JOHN Master Goche, I have a patient in Grafton whose condition troubled me greatly when I came away . . .

GOCHE Yes doctor . . . I understand the urgency you have to care for the body. Please understand the urgency I have to care for the soul! For I'm sure you agree that we must place the health of the soul above that of the body?

JOHN Of course.

(*He answers promptly, but does not like being required to.* SUSANNA *hides her thoughts.*)

GOCHE This last winter, in the dark months, there was an epidemic of the new fever . . . Ship Fever, I

believe some call it. Would you say it was
severe?

JOHN   Quite severe, yes.

GOCHE   How many deaths in Stratford?

JOHN   Around forty, I'd say . . .

GOCHE   And why does our merciful Lord send this new
                shivering plague over the seas to us, creeping
                across a cold land . . . to add to the summer
                plagues, the smallpox and the fevers we
                already have? Isn't it that his rising tide of
                death is to punish us for our infecting
                pestilence of sin? Isn't he saying that death
                itself is preferable to the death of the spirit?
                There are people walking these streets, within
                the shadow of this spire, who are dead inside
                their own bodies! The devil has sucked them
                dry. You say forty died in Stratford this
                winter? I'll show you four times forty who
                suffered the death of the soul. That is why we
                must reassert the authority of this court and
                all our church courts. For this is where the
                poisoned flood of moral and spiritual crime is
                held back where the disease is purged and
                bled! And so we dare not . . . must not . . .
                give anyone room to say this case went by
                default . . . that we may have closed it but they
                haven't . . . or that young Lane should hold
                forth to his drinking circle and say, "Well . . .
                it never got spoken, did it? But if I'd gone
                there . . . oh you'd have heard something."

SUSANNA   Your reverence . . . I'm confused. The charge
                was brought in my name and the bishop tells
                me I have won my case.

GOCHE   And now we must make your victory complete
                by eradicating all unfounded suspicion and
                rumour. For example, your husband wrote to
                the young man's father. People will ask . . .
                was this to strike some secret deal . . . to keep
                all discussion out of court?

JOHN	I said it would be better for his son if he confessed that his claims were false.
GOCHE	You suggested he plead guilty?
JOHN	(*facing up to it*) Yes.
GOCHE	Was there any inducement?
	(JOHN *decides on absolute truth.*)
JOHN	I said if the boy showed contrition I might help him.
GOCHE	"Might"?
JOHN	Would help him.
GOCHE	In what way?
JOHN	He wishes to study medicine. I couldn't take him back . . . but I would have enquired among other doctors if they would take him despite all this.
	(GOCHE *is interested.*)
GOCHE	You'd do so much?
JOHN	Providing my wife were able to forgive him . . .
SUSANNA	I hadn't thought of forgiveness until now. But, of course, if we show no intention to forgive we are not helping the sinner to repent. So I must.
GOCHE	He is excommunicated.
SUSANNA	Now . . . yes. So, I must wait for the church to be reconciled to him first.
	(GOCHE *realises she will not easily be cowed. He is more convinced that something is being hidden. He refers to his papers.*)
GOCHE	You know that the charges only contain part of his accusations against you? He claims, for

instance, that you prescribe medicines while your husband is absent.

SUSANNA   I have never prescribed medicines. What I have sometimes done is *make up* medicines that my husband has prescribed . . . but only if the apothecary is not with us, and only to my husband's instructions.

GOCHE   (*to* JOHN) Should a doctor's wife be involved in such matters?

JOHN   Master Goche, when I can't visit my patients . . . as I can't at this moment . . . I have to send instructions . . . in which case the patient's wife . . . or servant, or husband . . . is involved in such matters, let alone my wife. But, of course, Lane became angry that I trusted her exactness in weighing and measuring over his . . .

            (GOCHE *takes another document.*)

GOCHE   Let us look at some further claims made by Lane yesterday evening . . .

RAFE   Yesterday evening?

GOCHE   Yes, Master Smith.

RAFE   How can we know what he said yesterday evening?

GOCHE   Through the ears of the court, Master Smith. He claims . . . and I'm sure you would sooner this were answered than lie here unanswered . . . he claims that "Mistress Hall was as loose before marriage as within marriage and gave herself freely."

            (*Now* JOHN *is openly angry.*)

JOHN   My wife is here before you and you read her this!

            (RAFE *moves as though to exit.*)

RAFE   I can't listen to this. It's malice! Vengeance!

GOCHE   I want you to stay, Master Smith. I have
                questions for you later.

                (RAFE *stays*.)

JOHN   Why should we even have to consider this . . .
                gutter-talk?

GOCHE   It's defamation.

JOHN   It's dirt! Hardly fit for the sniggerers that we
                turn out from the back pew of the church . . .
                and you think it worth repeating here?

GOCHE   Remember I am the bishop's representative. I
                speak for him in law . . . and I decide what is
                or is not considered! But if at this point
                Mistress Hall wishes to retire and let you
                speak for her, so be it . . .

SUSANNA   No. I am the one it concerns . . .

JOHN   My wife is a good and honest and intelligent
                woman. Well, I'll say this plainly. When I
                first encountered her . . . the life and spirit
                she showed . . . I hardly dared believe that she
                could accept me for a husband. But God pitied
                me and was kind . . .

                (SUSANNA *and* RAFE *are, in their different
                ways, very affected by this.* GOCHE *watches
                them closely.*)

GOCHE   Did you not dare believe because she had
                many admirers who also were drawn to her
                'life and spirit'?

                (GOCHE *is trying to provoke the unguarded
                reply.* JOHN *becomes icily controlled.*)

JOHN   I want the bishop to attend this . . .
                discussion.

GOCHE   No sir! He vests his authority in me and is not
               to be called.

RAFE   He has said there is no stain on our
               characters!

GOCHE   And deputes me to support that with answers
               to all slanders made on you. Do you wish this
               to happen or don't you? It is for your good, the
               good of the law and the good of the church . . .

RAFE   (*indicates* JOHN) Don't seek to teach Dr Hall
               about the good of the church!

               (RAFE *expects a rebuke but does not get one.*)

GOCHE   No. (*To* JOHN.) I know of your work for Holy
               Trinity . . . and have heard of your hot
               arguments there . . . and I know you to hold
               views that I hold. I think we are of the same
               mind, doctor. It is for the Master Lanes of this
               world to issue unsubstantiated statements . . .
               not this court. Agreed?

               (JOHN *knows he has to stay.*)

SUSANNA   If my husband feels I can't stand the pain of
               hearing such things I assure him I'd sooner
               that than the pain of being in ignorance.
               Master Goche, I had a number of suitors
               before I eventually married . . . at twenty four.
               This was because I wished to remain and be a
               support for my mother . . . my father being so
               much away in London. The other reason was
               that, until my husband asked me, it was all too
               easy to say "no". So, if that is what you mean
               by 'admirers' . . .

GOCHE   How do we answer Lane's general claim?

SUSANNA   In the only way a 'general' claim can be
               answered by saying: this was not so. There are
               no particulars in it to be answered in any other
               way.

GOCHE   He becomes particular later . . . he said that
         on the second day of his staying at your house
         you kissed and embraced him on the stairs and
         called him "Sweet Jack".

         (JOHN . . . *and* RAFE . . . *are startled.*)

SUSANNA No. He did try to kiss me. I pushed him away
         and told him not to do it again . . . otherwise,
         (*She anticipates this one.*) I would have to tell
         my husband.

GOCHE   (*to* JOHN) Did she tell you?

         (JOHN *hesitates.*)

SUSANNA I had no need to, besides, I felt it was a young
         man being stupid and didn't wish to blight his
         future.

GOCHE   That was softness, Mistress Hall. Sin breeds in
         softness as maggots do!

         (SUSANNA'S *tone hardens slightly.*)

SUSANNA Yes Master Goche. But I have answered the
         claim.

GOCHE   And you never called him "Sweet Jack"?

SUSANNA Never.

GOCHE   Not even, at another time, perhaps . . . as a
         term of endearment?

SUSANNA Well, since he never actually endeared himself
         . . . no.

GOCHE   He says you are not easily detected in your
         amours because you inherit from your father
         the art of dissembling. He is of the theatre, is
         he not?

SUSANNA I know you will hold that against him, Master
         Goche. Please do not hold it against me.

GOCHE   (*coldly*) He acts . . . so he dissembles. What
             d'you say to the claim that you may do so?

SUSANNA   Since I am answering all the other claims
             there is nothing to dissemble about.

GOCHE   Good. Good. My own father was a poet,
             religious verse. We are not so far apart as you
             may think. I am here to help you.

             (*He smiles apparent approval of her answer
             but is deliberately softening the tone to get
             her off guard.*)

             To return to his original claims. As to the first
             . . . the running of the reins . . .

JOHN   You have their denial. I support it . . . but
             they will see any physician anyone cares to
             name.

GOCHE   Quite. As to the second claim, Mistress Hall, I
             simply have to ask, did you meet Master
             Smith, alone, at John Palmer's house and
             there commit the sin of carnality?

SUSANNA   I did not.

GOCHE   And Master Smith . . . the same question.

             (RAFE *is now very tense.*)

RAFE   Mistress Hall has answered.

GOCHE   I need you to answer as well.

RAFE   The same. . . no.

GOCHE   Did you go to John Palmer's that night?

             (RAFE *can't think whether it is best to confirm
             or deny.*)

RAFE   That night?

GOCHE   You held the key . . . and since the house was
           empty you may well have gone to see that all
           was well . . .

           (GOCHE *appears to help him. Since he is
           convinced that any liaison happened at Hall's
           house, he is not interested in Palmer's.*)

RAFE   Yes. I did that. As you say . . . to see . . .

GOCHE   And then did you go home?

RAFE   Yes.

GOCHE   Could someone confirm it . . . ? Your wife,
           perhaps . . .

RAFE   My wife must not be asked! Her mind is not in
           a state of balance. We lost two children with
           the fever.

GOCHE   I'm sorry to hear it. But are you aware that
           your wife has confided to neighbours that she
           believes you lusted after Mistress Hall?

RAFE   It's her mind. I've just told you . . . her mind!
           She's much given to invention and rejecting
           those around her . . .

JOHN   I have treated Mistress Smith for her
           melancholy fits. Questioning would worsen
           her condition. In such cases the patient should
           not be troubled.

GOCHE   But there are others who will say you thought
           impurely of Mistress Hall and how will we
           answer that?

RAFE   My thoughts? I'm to answer for my thoughts?

GOCHE   Yes, sir.

RAFE   What is to be gained by this? A man can state
           his thoughts and another can disbelieve him.
           Who's to decide? My thoughts are between me
           and God!

(RAFE *is losing control.* SUSANNA *and* JOHN *are increasingly alarmed. Suddenly* RAFE *sees a way of answering 'truthfully'.*)

No! No! I never thought impurely of her . . . never!

(GOCHE *is well aware of his wriggling.*)

GOCHE   I think the only way to deal with this is to make the question ultimate and categoric. We are doing God's work and must scour the cauldron clean. Have you ever, in any place and at any time, had carnal knowledge of Mistress Hall?

(RAFE *pounces on this with his rehearsed answer.*)

RAFE   No! That I can totally deny. No!

GOCHE   You answer me strangely. Have you committed the lesser sins of lechery? Have you ever seen her naked or touched her flesh?

(SUSANNA *gasps and sways to distract from* RAFE *having to answer.* JOHN, *too, has mixed motives in intervening.*)

JOHN   This is too far! You are attacking the honour of my wife!

GOCHE   No doctor. I am seeking to prevent others from doing so!

SUSANNA   Master Goche, I have tried to show no weakness through all that has been said. I recognise that what you have to do is for our protection. But surely there has to be room in all of this for trust? You speak of sin. May I name one virtue: to think well of others. See the good in them before counting their faults. Even young Master Lane I saw first as benign and generous to his fellow creatures. But he is

too easily crossed . . . behaves stupidly . . .
more misguided and wayward than evil. And
surely, surely, in making wild claims against
me or Master Smith with no speck of evidence
he only condemns himself in people's eyes and
lapses from the qualities he has. He's a figure
of pity now. Our evidence empties his claims
and leaves him nothing.

GOCHE   You must not presume to think you know the
extent of the dark kingdom, Mistress Hall, or
the furthest reach of Satan's grasp. Even here
in the shadows of this holy place he can stand
breathing at our shoulder. He has entered into
Master Lane . . . ravished his soul . . . left him
wasted . . . so that even his companions sense
that he is consumed. I can always tell . . .
when so many report so freely on a man. They
wish to save themselves and store up credit
with the Lord. They hold back from him,
fearing to slip into the throat of Hell!

(JOHN *inwardly disapproves the zealous tone of
this*.)

JOHN   It seems to me, Master Goche, you have all
you need. We ride slowly. We should make our
move.

GOCHE   Then tell me . . . is there anything that has not
been said that I ought to know . . . anything
that could be seized on by Lane, or anyone, to
undermine the court's proclamation of your
innocence? (*An uneasy moment.* RAFE *is the
most vulnerable — and* GOCHE *can see it.*)
Then we'll examine one more item and then
I've done. Master Smith . . . after Dr Hall rode
to Shipston you visited Mistress Hall twice . . .
once to invite her to supper . . . and, on a
second visit that night, to withdraw that
invitation?

RAFE   To explain it . . . to explain. My wife . . . she
couldn't . . .

GOCHE   Yes, I understand. Mistress Hall, in your
               deposition . . . (*He refers to his papers.*) . . .
               you say that your servant, Hester, can testify
               that she saw him arrive and depart on the first
               occasion. On the second visit she saw him
               depart . . . (*Reads.*) "by the side gate" . . . but
               it is not clear that she was present to see him
               arrive. Did she see him arrive?

               (SUSANNA *thinks carefully.*)

SUSANNA   Yes . . .

GOCHE   You hesitated.

SUSANNA   I was thinking back . . .

GOCHE   We must be sure. I want no one to be able to
               suggest that Master Smith was ever alone with
               you. He was never alone with you was he?

               (SUSANNA *knows they are dealing with a gap in*
               HESTER'S *testimony . . . but in* HESTER'S
               absence she determines to close it.)

SUSANNA   No. Never.

GOCHE   So your servant must have seen him arrive?

SUSANNA   Yes.

               (GOCHE *makes a move to look down the nave of
               the cathedral.*)

GOCHE   Then we will hear her confirm that and the
               whole matter is concluded . . .

JOHN   She's not with us. I sent her ahead to the inn
               to make things ready.

GOCHE   Yes . . . I saw her leaving. She was told to
               wait. (*He beckons to* HESTER *offstage.*) Come!

               (HESTER *enters, but with a determination and
               defiance we have not seen before. She is angry
               at her treatment and rubs her wrist, which is*

hurt. SUSANNA, JOHN *and* RAFE *are horrified to see her.*)

JOHN   You detained my servant with no reference to
                me!

GOCHE   This is a court sir! She is a witness.

JOHN   The court is not in session!

GOCHE   But it is here . . . in session or not! D'you
                think God's justice is turned on and off like a
                tap? Now, I want no one to speak to her while
                she testifies . . .

JOHN   One moment . . .

GOCHE   Dr Hall!

JOHN   Hester . . . why d'you rub your wrist?

HESTER   A man held me by the wrists to stop me
                leaving. I said you'd given me orders to go to
                the inn but he wouldn't let me . . .

JOHN   You had her kept here by force?

GOCHE   There would have been no need if she'd
                obeyed the court officer. I'll speak to the man
                . . . but we must resolve this first. Hester, look
                at me and keep looking at me. Are you
                truthful?

HESTER   Yes, your worship . . .

GOCHE   Look up at the roof . . .

HESTER   I can't your worship . . .

GOCHE   Look up!

                (*She does so, fearfully . . . then seems to 'see'
                something that calms her and strengthens her
                resolve.*)

                That is God listening to you, Hester.

HESTER   Yes . . . dear Lord!

(She smiles round at the others in an assuring way that puzzles them.)

GOCHE   Look at me. Don't look away. I want you to think back to the day the doctor went to Shipston. You had taken the child, Elizabeth, to her grandparents at New Place. You returned in the dark with Master Lane . . .

HESTER   No your worship . . . not with him. He was following me . . . I was trying to hurry away from him.

GOCHE   But he caught up with you and entered Dr Hall's house with you . . .

HESTER   Yes, your worship.

GOCHE   He waited in the porch . . .

HESTER   He had to sit down sir . . . he was in a state . . .

GOCHE   And you went into the garden?

HESTER   Yes, your worship.

GOCHE   And who did you see?

HESTER   Master Smith with Mistress Hall.

(GOCHE confronts SUSANNA.)

GOCHE   Well, Mistress Hall . . . Hester *didn't* see Master Smith arrive!

(HESTER quickly detects the situation.)

HESTER   Yes I did, your worship. Before I got to the house I was running to get ahead of Master Lane and I saw Master Smith in front of me and he turned and went in at the side gate . . . he usually used the gate . . . the same way he went when he left.

(She sounds totally truthful. GOCHE is thrown off balance a moment.)

GOCHE	How did you recognise him in the dark?
HESTER	Oh . . . there was a moon . . . it was like day! And he has a way of opening the gate . . . pulls it sharp towards him first because the latch doesn't lift easily. So you hear a bump . . . then two sharp clicks . . . only he does it. I've known that sound for years!

(*She smiles at* RAFE, *who is half fearful and half fascinated by her easy lying.*)

GOCHE	Master Lane doesn't say he saw him.
HESTER	He was a good way behind me . . . I think he'd stumbled.
GOCHE	You then went into the house by the main door?
HESTER	Yes, your worship.
GOCHE	Is that nearer than the side gate?
HESTER	No . . . further . . .
GOCHE	Then why not go to the side gate!
HESTER	I was holding my key. I had this thought that I'd lead Master Lane to the front then ask the mistress's permission to lock the door against him . . . but suddenly he'd caught up with me and got in . . .
GOCHE	How did you know that your mistress would be at home when the last time you were with her she had been asked away to supper?
HESTER	Because an hour before I had gone round to bring back milk from the evening milking to New Place . . . and I stopped and listened. It was very still and I could hear the sound of the bellows working in the furnace . . . there's a small furnace in the dispensary . . . you need fire . . . you have to have heat for the precious

stones . . . and I knew it was her . . . working like she sometimes does. So I thought what I'd thought all along, that the supper might not happen . . . that Mistress Smith . . . might not be able . . .

(GOCHE *gathers up his papers, resigned to defeat.*)

GOCHE   There is much I could ask . . . but I will conclude this business.

(*He takes the attitude of prayer.*)

Oh Lord, we will make today a proclamation of the innocence of thy servants, Mistress Susanna Hall and Master Rafe Smith. Bless this work we do in thy name, through Jesus Christ our Saviour . . . Amen.

(*He prepares to go.*)

Carry the word to your parish congregation that the consistory court at Worcester has done with leniency and bungling. The moral void of our times . . . the retreat from grace . . . demand that justice uses a sharper sword. I know you'd expect nothing less, Dr Hall. Tell them that those who commit contempt . . . or perjury . . . (*He lets this sink in.*) . . . will not only put their souls on the everlasting rack but, if I have my way, will face the utmost that the civil courts can do to whip it and jail it out of them.

(*He exits, still suspecting that something may have been hidden from him.* SUSANNA *hides her inner triumph. The men are spent. Slowly* HESTER *sinks to the floor, still smiling but emotionally exhausted.*)

HESTER   I saw God . . . up in the roof . . . and I was so glad! For I could see that he wanted me to lie!

(HESTER *begins to shake.* SUSANNA *embraces her. Fade to black.*)

Scene Three

The garden at DOCTOR HALL'S, *as before, some weeks later. Evening. The squeaking of bats.*

We discover JACK LANE, *dishevelled, dirty and on his way to becoming — as he became — the town drunk. He knocks at the dispensary door and calls out.*

JACK   Doctor! Doctor! Dr Hall! Don't shun me
              doctor. Don't turn your back. I'm down. I'm
              flat! What do I do? Beg and go barefoot? Oh
              the horror of doing such wrong. Mistress . . .
              mistress . . . was it me? But what's the good of
              penance in a white sheet? Let me do penance
              to you. And to you doctor. Let me work off my
              sin! I'll be your rag man . . . wipe up the
              vomit and the puss, the bloody flux and
              phlegm and stinking stools! Anything! I'll
              wash lepers . . . poultice tumours . . . spread
              ointment on swollen, syphillitic cods . . .
              bathe running gout. And all of it would shine
              like clear spring water compared with the filth
              that I spewed up!

              (HESTER *appears at the dispensary door.*)

HESTER   We'll give you three minutes and I'll call Tom
              to you . . .

JACK   Call him. I'll Tom him. Hey Hester . . . is
              there anything wet in there?

              (SUSANNA *appears beside* HESTER.)

SUSANNA   (*to* HESTER) You get on with the room. I'll
              speak to him.

HESTER   You shouldn't have to!

SUSANNA   But I will.

(HESTER *disappears into the house.*)

(*to* JACK) I'm amazed you come here . . .

JACK	To make amends, mistress . . . I'm being punished all ends up. I've no money.
SUSANNA	I know you haven't.
JACK	Nowhere to sleep. I sleep in barns.
SUSANNA	Well that's somewhere. No . . . no more. I don't believe any of it. It's all stories.
JACK	Well you're the one for stories . . .

(SUSANNA *stops smiling.*)

SUSANNA	We need some peace now. Please go.
JACK	You kissed me once. You called me "Sweet Jack" . . . you say you didn't but you did.
SUSANNA	Well, if you want to think so, think so . . .
JACK	And your eyes . . . when they looked.

(*Enter* RAFE *by the garden gate.*)

RAFE	Out!
JACK	No . . . no.
RAFE	Out on the street!
JACK	I've pawned my sword so you've nothing to fear . . .
RAFE	Find a gutter and stay in it!
SUSANNA	Let him go peacefully . . . none of this.
JACK	No, I mean . . . bygones . . .

(*He offers his hand.* RAFE *ignores it.*)

Touch it if you won't shake it. I think we'd have hit it off well, you and I . . .

RAFE	This creature! This louse!
SUSANNA	Quietly . . .
JACK	(*still offering hand*) Tap it then. Just a tap to say we shared something once. You remember, in the river? Yeeooo that water was cold! But him!
	(*He points at* RAFE.)
	Oh mistress . . . what I could say!
	(*He exits.*)
RAFE	I came to tell you they're ready.
SUSANNA	And we're ready. The room's ready. But I wish John were here.
	(*She goes to the dispensary and checks a pan of simmering liquid on the embers of the fire.* RAFE *wrestles with what he wants to tell her.*)
RAFE	This time next week . . . I've made up my mind. I'll set out. I'll go.
SUSANNA	What's this?
RAFE	I'll leave her well provided. She can have it all!
SUSANNA	Rafe . . . we're getting tired of hearing you . . .
RAFE	I'll walk to Bristol. I've a cousin there. He'll help me find a ship.
SUSANNA	What do you know of ships?
RAFE	They'll take me. They'll take anything that crawls!
	(*She comes to him.*)
SUSANNA	You mustn't say these things . . .
RAFE	We lied to God!

SUSANNA   How can you lie to God when he knows
            everything? You can only lie to someone who
            doesn't know the truth. God knows the truth
            and he knows many truths. He knows that it is
            true that I love you Rafe . . . for all your
            storms. But he also knows it is true that I care
            deeply for John and respect him. Both are
            true. One doesn't rule out the other. In God's
            eyes they go side by side . . . and he sees how
            John loves you . . .

RAFE   Hates!

SUSANNA   Loves and wants you here. He knows what you
            went through for him.

            (HESTER *enters from the house.*)

HESTER   It's all done.

SUSANNA   Do we have barley?

HESTER   Yes. Plenty.

SUSANNA   Hartshorn . . . plantain . . . betony?

            (HESTER *nods to them all.*)

HESTER   Does the fire need anything?

SUSANNA   Just a little.

            (*Before* HESTER *can go to the furnace,* RAFE,
            *wanting to do something, crosses and uses the
            bellows.*)

HESTER   (*aside*) How is he?

SUSANNA   At war . . .

HESTER   Not thinking of going?

SUSANNA   As ever . . .

HESTER   (*rueful, wishing for him as a husband*) Oh if
            only . . .

            (*They share the thought.*)

SUSANNA   If only, if only, if only . . . it'd make a good
               song. (*They hear a horse coming to the
               stable.*) John!

               (HESTER *runs into the house.* RAFE *moves to the
               gate.*)

RAFE   I'll leave . . .

SUSANNA   No . . . he wants you here. He doesn't want
               you to stop coming. You must show the town
               there's no rift between us.

               (JOHN *enters, weary and dusty from riding. He
               hides any misgivings and greets* RAFE *well.*)

JOHN   Rafe . . . I'm glad to see you.

               (*He takes* SUSANNA'S *hands and kisses them,
               nodding his assurance that it's alright for*
               RAFE *to be with her.*)

SUSANNA   Rafe's here to help. It's father . . . he's agreed
               to be brought over to us. We've got the room
               ready.

JOHN   Is he worse?

SUSANNA   The same. No better . . .

               (JOHN *winces as he sits.*)

JOHN   I'm raw. I should buy a new saddle. I'm
               practically growing a saddle on me!

SUSANNA   Are you bleeding?

JOHN   I daresay . . .

SUSANNA   The ointment?

JOHN   (*self-hating*) Let it bleed!

               (HESTER *enters with drinks and cakes.*)

               Thank you, Hester.

(She exits.)

RAFE   I'll go round and see what stage they're at . . .

JOHN   Rafe . . . you're not going to leave us?

RAFE   Just to look how things are . . .

(RAFE has deliberately avoided the meaning. JOHN pursues it.)

JOHN   Not leave here . . . and go from us?

(RAFE accepts the meaning.)

RAFE   I don't know. *(Then determinedly.)* Yes.

(He exits through the side gate.)

JOHN   You must pursuade him. *(He challenges her with this. She remains silent.)* Your father . . . did he have the tincture for the ulcers? *(She nods.)* That night, when you had out the Venetian turpentine potion and the lead box . . . and the rest . . . you intended them for him, didn't you?

(It goes hard with SUSANNA to admit that she suspected her father of having gonorrhea.)

SUSANNA   It's what I thought he had then, yes.

JOHN   You must know . . . he's far beyond that now.

SUSANNA   Yes.

JOHN   I've been wondering how God would punish me. What? Take the lies that flew out of my mouth . . . make them birds of prey, to feed on my own flesh for all eternity? No . . . he does something far, far simpler. He brings me face to face with my own ignorance. And it comes grinning at me now! For suddenly here's the father of my own wife desperate for cure and here am I . . . helpless!

SUSANNA   Not helpless. Never helpless!

JOHN   I let us do what we did to protect my practice!
              Now God shows me what a piece of pride and
              arrogance that was!

SUSANNA   Is God so cold? He gives . . . not takes away!
              And the greatest gift is to have the will to help
              . . . no matter how helpless we may feel!

              (*She crosses to the dispensary to check the
              simmering liquid.*)

              I've boiled the potion.

JOHN   No! It's not for you to be doing . . . we shall
              be watched . . .

              (*But* SUSANNA *gives him a look of quiet
              determination.*)

SUSANNA   John. We have a bond between us now . . . you
              and I. We know what has to be done.

              (RAFE *enters from the side gate.*)

RAFE   They've set out. They have him on a litter . . .
              it's too wide for the door or the gate. Shall we
              use a chair?

              (JOHN, *still trying to take in his wife's attitude,
              doesn't respond.*)

              A chair to carry him into the house?

              (*We see* JACK LANE *looking in at the gate as*
              SUSANNA *replies for* JOHN.)

SUSANNA   Yes . . . a chair. We'll use the carver . . .
              Hester!

RAFE   I'll bring it.

              (*He crosses to the house and exits.* JACK *comes
              forward.*)

JACK   Let me help . . . I'll be his chair carrier,
                mistress! Use me! You won't say me nay,
                doctor, will you?

                (*Getting no reply, he runs to the house where
                he almost collides with* HESTER *and* RAFE
                carrying out a large carver chair.)

                I'll do it!

                (*He tries to take over from* HESTER *who angrily
                resists.*)

HESTER   No!

SUSANNA   (*to* HESTER) Let him . . . (*Then.*) Get pillows
                and a blanket, quickly!

                (HESTER *returns to the house.* JACK *eagerly
                bears the front of the chair.* RAFE, *furious, at
                the back of it.*)

JACK   We'll bear him mistress . . . Rafe and me.

                (*As* JACK *pauses to ingratiate himself with
                them,* RAFE *urges him on.*)

RAFE   Through the gate! Through the gate.

                (*They exit through the gate.* HESTER *comes
                from the house with pillows, blanket and
                lantern. She exits after them.* JOHN *and*
                SUSANNA *are left face to face.* JOHN *accepts
                that, lack of knowledge or not, he must do
                what he can. He nods and touches her on the
                shoulder . . . then exits through the gate to
                join the others.* SUSANNA *doesn't follow. She
                looks around for some excuse for not going
                out to see her father arrive. She goes to the
                dispensary and slowly pumps the furnace. In
                the gathering darkness it glows. She watches
                the liquid boil in the pan.* HESTER *re-enters.*)

HESTER   They're at the corner . . . shall I take that up?

SUSANNA   Yes.

              (HESTER *gets a cloth to hold the pan.*)

HESTER   We'll take care of him . . .

SUSANNA   He was a liar, too. Must have lied to my
              mother every time he came home. Yet when he
              was with us . . . we were so warm!

              (*As* HESTER *takes the pan,* SUSANNA *looks up
              again at the sky.*)

              Well . . . leave coldness to the stars. Give us
              life . . .

              (*They both turn to face the gate as we hear
              the voices beyond.*)

JOHN   (*off*) Easy . . . take the legs . . . gently.

RAFE   (*off*) Turn him now . . .

JOHN   (*off*) Gently . . . gently . . .

THE END